ACTIVITIES

Scientific Enquiry

AGES 5–7

GEORGIE BEASLEY
ROGER SMITH

Authors
Georgie Beasley
Roger Smith

Editors
Caroline Carless
Sally Gray

Project Editor
Fabia Lewis

Series Designers
Anthony Long
Joy Monkhouse

Designer
Catherine Perera

Illustrations
Garry Davis

Photographs
Peter Rowe

Published by Scholastic Ltd,
Villiers House,
Clarendon Avenue,
Leamington Spa,
Warwickshire CV32 5PR

www.scholastic.co.uk

Designed using Adobe Indesign

Printed by Tien Wah Press Ltd, Singapore

1 2 3 4 5 6 7 8 9   7 8 9 0 1 2 3 4 5 6

British Library Cataloguing-in-Publication Data

A catalogue record for this book is available from the British Library.

ISBN 978-0439-94500-4

Contents

Introduction

When science is taught well, it provides a framework for children to develop both skills and knowledge. For them to do this effectively, it is essential that they observe, explore and ask questions about living things, materials and phenomena in as creative a way as possible, because it is in through the *doing* of the science, that they will learn best.

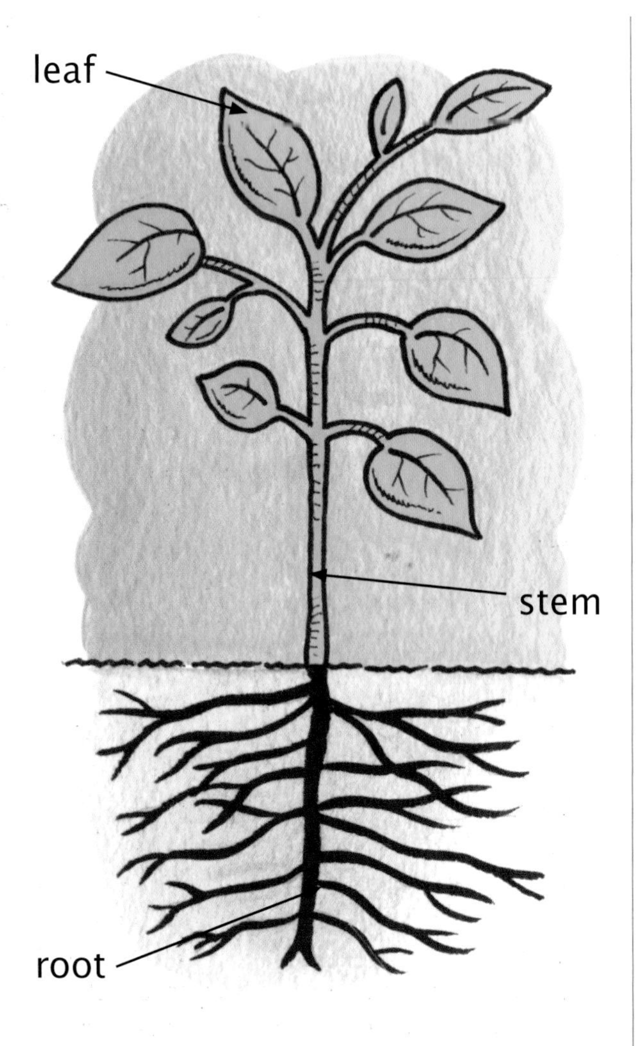

Each of the activities uses the same structure that sets objectives and lays out what you and the children have to do, using step by step headings and providing useful photocopiable resources. At the same time, the activities are both adaptable and imaginative and encourage the children to solve problems, think independently and work flexibly. Most of the activities can easily stand alone as they illustrate specific objectives, but they can also be used as part of a series of lessons, on a particular subject. Thoughtful planning and integration into your science curriculum will mean that you are able to develop the kind of creativity that these activities encourage, and once you have chosen which problem to solve, it is relatively easy to:

- Encourage open-ended questions
- Reward imagination and originality
- Increase the children's use of hands-on experimentation
- Encourage problem-solving
- Develop skills in collaborative group work
- Create conditions for the exploration of ideas
- Encourage quiet reflection and concentration
- Stand back, when appropriate and let the children take the lead

Some of the scientific concepts, for example, reflection, sound waves and how rainbows are created are quite difficult to understand without practical experience but, at the same time, they will be better understood if there are opportunities for questions, answers and discussions about specific concepts. Effective science teaching is about balancing the 'theoretical' and the 'practical' and finding the right task to meet the objectives of the curriculum. All this is made easier at Key Stage 1 because young children are naturally curious about the world they live in and how it all fits together.

All the activities can be adapted to suit most classrooms and the required materials should either be readily available or can be

© Peter Rowe Coins ©The Royal Mint

bought cheaply and easily. Some activities will need more precise teacher instructions and a more structured approach than others. Many activities are deliberately open-ended and will depend largely on how far the children are able to use their imaginations and perseverance. Specific skills will gradually become more and more important because science is essentially about collecting evidence, making observations and measurements and trying to use previous knowledge and skills to answer scientific questions.

When working on a particular activity, children should be encouraged to explore different strategies and make decisions about how to record outcomes. Each activity is set in an imaginary context in order to ensure it is presented in a relevant and interesting way and the children should be encouraged to take part in the fantasy scenarios. They should empathise with the lighthouse keeper, who desperately wants his lunch; they should want to help the struggling artist Will Daubalot and they should see themselves as being really helpful in solving the problems that the imaginary characters have.

Different groups of children may respond to the problems in different ways and it may be necessary to adapt the suggested plans to meet the needs of a particular group of learners. Each problem should appeal to different learning styles and there are opportunities for many varied responses.

Also, each activity can, if required, be seen as a complete unit – a single lesson that illustrates a specific scientific concept but they can also be used much more flexibly. Activities can be linked to other subject areas such as, art and design technology. They can also incorporate all kinds of printed materials and multimedia resources for interactive whiteboards and PCs. This will encourage children to look deeper or wider into similar themes and activities.

Because the activities are practical, it would be helpful to have as many support assistants as possible in the classroom. Some activities require materials that need a certain amount of extra care for example, washing-up liquid and food colouring. Some of the activities may take several weeks to complete and therefore need careful forward planning.

Chapter Five: Electricity, light and sound

Hot weather

Setting the context

It was the hottest summer on record and it was only June. How was Mary going to cope with the heat? She had no aircooling system in her house because usually it wasn't needed. Anyway, it would be good to have something that she could carry around with her, so she could use it when she was inside or outside. What could she use to keep herself cool?

The problem

How can we help Mary make a hand-held device that would help keep her cool?

Page 82

Objectives

To find out about simple **circuits** involving **batteries**, wires and motors.

To learn how a switch can be used to break a circuit.

You will need

Different kinds of hand held, non-… fans; paper; stapler and staples; … scissors; **electrical** kits to make a … with wire, a switch, batteries and …

Preparation

Cut the paper to the right size for making hand-held, non-motorised fans. Organise the electrical equipment into sets so that each pair of children has enough to make a circuit to include a motor. Check that each set works, before the session!

Discussion and research

- Brainstorm all the different ways we can keep cool during very hot weather.
- Collect the ones that will help keep Mary cool easily when she is inside and out.
- Agree that she needs a hand-held device of some sort to keep cool.
- Give the children one minute to discuss with a partner their ideas for hand-held devices, before collecting their ideas.

Obtaining evidence

- Depending on the children's ideas, invite each child to make a fan by folding paper. Let each group look at one already made first, to work out how the design works before making one each by folding paper in a concertina style and stapling one end.
- Hold a mini-review to try out the fans. As the children fan themselves, talk about how they were made and whether they are efficient. How long do the children think they could keep this up? Either ask the children: *Can anyone come up with a better idea?* or *How can we make one of those fans that spin around* **automatically**? If this has already been suggested.
- Get out the equipment and let the children make a hand-held fan that works with a battery. They will need to think of a design for the fans to stick to the end of the motor.
- Ask them to put a switch into the circuit so they can turn the fan on and off.

Drawing together

- Try out the battery-operated fans. Decide whether these are better.
- Look at a commercial battery-operated fan and decide what the mechanism inside will look like. *Who thinks it will be similar to the circuits you have made?*

Support

Help some of the children make their circuit so that they do not short circuit it and burn out the battery.

Extension

When the children have made their own battery-operated fans, ask the more confident learners to consider how a large, electrically-operated fan works. … them to draw what they think the inside looks like.

Scientific language

electrical – works by electricity.

circuit – wires and a battery providing a small amount of electricity to make something such as a bulb, buzzer or motor work.

battery – small object that provides small amounts of electricity.

automatic – works without a human action.

Page 83

Creative Activities for Scientific Enquiry: Ages 5-7

Each activity has a certain degree of challenge and the problems can be adapted to suit children of all levels of ability by using the 'Support', 'Extension' and 'Further ideas' sections. What the activities should really do, if used positively and creatively, is excite the children and make them want to discover more about the complex world that they live in – the world they will ultimately grow up to change!

Chapter One

Humans and other animals

The six activities in this chapter are designed to teach children about the different features of humans and other animals, and about the environments and diets that they require for survival.

Who stole the tart? encourages children to identify the external features which human beings have in common and those which can be used to distinguish between different individuals. This is carried out through the comparison of photographs, in the context of solving a mystery.

Who's been eating my boot? presents the children with another mystery, which can be solved by learning about the types and features of animals that are found in their local environment. It particularly focuses on gathering evidence through visual clues.

In **Farmer Giles**, children are introduced to the idea that some animals produce their offspring by laying eggs. The activity in this lesson requires them to identify which eggs belong to which animals, using both reference materials and real eggs as visual aids.

Mother Hubbard's bare cupboard focuses on the importance of a healthy, nutritious and varied diet for human beings. The lesson stimulates discussion of which foods and drinks are healthy or less healthy, followed by an opportunity for the children to design nutritionally balanced meals.

Animal hide-and-seek is designed to help children understand why certain animals are suited to living in certain environments, and the different conditions that animals require in order to survive. It also introduces the concept of camouflage as a means of hiding.

The experiment in **Bird table** involves finding out which type of bird food attracts the most birds. In addition to teaching children about birds and their feeding habits, it also requires them to make predictions, think about how to set up a fair test and compare their results to their predictions at the end of the activity.

Who stole the tart?

Setting the context

Andy's grandmother thought she was living in a nursery rhyme. She had made a batch of lemon curd tarts only that morning because they were Andy's favourite and he was coming for tea. She had put them by the open window to cool and when she went to put them onto a plate ready for tea, she found that one was missing. Fortunately her neighbour saw the person who did it, but he could not speak because he had laryngitis. He could only nod or shake his head.

The problem

How can Andy's grandmother find out who stole the tart?

Objectives

To be able to make simple comparisons.
To learn to recognise and compare external parts of the body and features of humans.
To know how to group living things according to observable similarities and differences.

You will need

Photographs of people with different **features** such as hair colour, length and style, eye colour, with and without freckles, wearing glasses and not and so on; large sheets of paper and felt-tipped pens; card to add questions.

Preparation

Take photographs or cut out pictures from published magazines of a range of people.

Discussion and research

- Introduce the problem.
- Ask the children what they need to find out. What information will they need to have about the person?
- Summarise their suggestions by saying, for example, *So we need to know whether the person is male or female, how tall they are, how old they are and what they look like.*
- Ask the children to talk with a partner to make suggestions as to how they can help Andy's grandmother find out who the culprit is, if the neighbour cannot speak.
- Listen and respond to the children's ideas.
- If the children do not come up with the idea of asking questions that require a yes or no answer, point this out.

Obtaining evidence

- Organise the children into groups of five or six. Give each group a picture and give them no more than five minutes to talk about what the person in their picture looks like.
- As a whole class, ask one child from each group to describe their picture. Encourage the use of words that describe gender, age, size, eye and hair colour and any distinguishing features that will help.
- Make a list of these on a large sheet of paper.
- Give the children ten minutes to work in their groups to make a list of questions.
- Share the questions so far. Put those that are useful in a list down the side of a

© Peter Rowe

whiteboard and discard those that are not.

- Choose a couple of questions and ask the children to say what this tells us about the person if the answer is yes and then if the answer is no.
- Record this to the right of the question. For example, if the question is, 'Does the person have blue eyes?' and the answer is yes, then we know that the person has blue eyes; if the answer is no, then the person has green or brown eyes.

Drawing together

- Ask the children to return to their groups and transfer the questions onto cards.
- Use a set of questions to act out the conversation between Andy's grandmother and her neighbour.
- Ask the person playing the neighbour to choose one of the people in the pictures to be the culprit.
- The person playing the grandmother should then ask his or her questions.
- After each question, use a decision tree to eliminate certain people and to eventually find out which person stole the tart.

Support

Ask an adult to help the children to develop the language they need to describe the features and to act as a scribe to record the questions.

Extension

With the more confident learners, talk about which questions will be the most useful and least useful. Put them in order according to whether they eliminate more or fewer people. Challenge them to find the culprit using only five questions.

Scientific language

features – part of the face, especially regarding shape and looks.

Who's been eating my boot?

Setting the context

I went into the school garden this morning and found that one of my favourite wellington boots had a hole in its toe. Someone or something had chewed their way through to the inside and removed some of the warm lining. Whatever it was it left some clues.

The problem

How can we find out who chewed the hole in the boot?

Objectives

To learn to decide how to find answers to questions.
To know about the senses that enable humans to be aware of the world around them.
To find out about the different animals in the local environment.

You will need

A photograph of the wellington boot with a hole chewed through and the outer material spread around the outside; a set of pictures or photos for each group of **footprints** of animals found in the local environment, and if possible in a format for displaying on an interactive whiteboard or screen, if you have access to one; reference materials for the children to find the animals that match the footprints.

Preparation

Leave a trail of clues in the school garden that will require the children to use their sense of sight to track down the culprit. Include footprints of several different animals such as a deer, cat, dog, bird and hedgehog. You will need to dampen down some soil and mark these with a suitable garden tool or stick. Make sure the trail runs cold when it reaches a stone path or grassy lawn. Leave

some warm fabric, similar to the inside of the wellington boot, arranged as a nest under a hedge.

Discussion and research

- Tell the children the story of finding the wellington boot with a hole chewed through it. Emphasise that the culprit left some teeth marks.
- Show them the photo and talk about the crime scene.
- Ask the following questions: *What do we already know? What does the photo tell us about the animal that caused the damage? What was the animal looking for? How do you know?*
- List all the animals that could have caused the damage. Throw in some silly questions, for example;*Could it have been a tiger? Why not?* This will encourage the children to suggest only animals that they know can be found in the local environment.

Obtaining evidence

- Ask the children: *What do we still need to find out? How can we find this out?*
- Give the children the pictures of the footprints and give them ten minutes to identify which animal each could belong to.
- Look at the footprints together, using those displayed on the whiteboard if you have one, and for each one agree which animal it could be, and whether it can be found in the local environment and therefore could be the culprit.
- Tell the children that they are detectives who are going to try to find the animal that caused the damage. Ask them which of their senses they are going to use. *Why is the sense of sight the most useful in this investigation?*
- Go outside and follow the clues until the children find the nest, under the hedge.

Drawing together

- On return to the classroom, ask the children: *Who could own the nest*? Identify the animals which would build such a nest.
- *Could it belong to a bird?* Deduce with the children that a bird does not have teeth, so could not have left the teeth marks.
- Discuss how to decide to which animal the nest belongs.

Support

Work with the children to help them identify the footprints. Talk about the shape and the size. Work with them outside to point out the prints.

Extension

Ask the children to give reasons for their decisions; for example, the animal's size and shape. Ask them to say which other animals, for which we do not have clues, could have chewed the hole.

Scientific language

footprints – marks left on the ground in the same shape as the features on the bottom of an animal's foot.

Farmer Giles

Setting the context

Farmer Giles, who lives about 20 miles away from the school, went to check his crops one morning. As he walked around his field, he noticed an egg lying in one corner and he couldn't return it because he did not know what animal to look for.

The problem

How can we help the farmer return the egg to its owner?

Objectives

To be able to use simple information sources to find answers to questions.
To know that animals produce offspring that grow into the same adult animals.
To learn to relate life processes to animals found in the local environment.
To know to treat animals with care and sensitivity.

You will need

A hen's **egg** and a duck or goose egg; pictures of different sized and coloured eggs that could be found in the local environment; access to the internet or reference books showing different types of eggs and related adults.

Preparation

It would be useful if the children have had experience of asking scientific questions and have completed some work on the animals that are likely to be found in their local environment.

Discussion and research

- Tell the children the problem and identify what we already know and what we need to find out.
- Ask the children to suggest a way of finding the answer to the problem. Identify the animals that produce their young by laying eggs.

Obtaining evidence

- Put the children into groups and give each one a picture of a different size and colour of egg to research.
- Use the reference material to find the matching adult and write a short description to help the farmer look for the right animal and know where to look to find them.

Drawing together

- Gather together and share each other's

descriptions. Did the children find any other animals that could have laid the egg that are not represented by the eggs researched so far?

- Identify the animals that can be found in the local area and those that cannot.
- How do the children think their animal came to lay an egg in Farmer Giles's field?

Support

Give some children an actual duck or goose egg to research. First, talk to them about a familiar hen's egg and compare this with the one that they have. Talk about the size, shape and colour. Note the similarities and differences between the eggs before finding out which animal owns their egg.

Extension

Give the children pictures of eggs, belonging to animals that come from a contrasting environment, to research; for example, an ostrich egg or a **reptile** egg.

Scientific language

egg – laid by some animals and containing what it needs to grow into a new animal of the same type.

reptile – crawling animal that hatches from an egg.

Mother Hubbard's bare cupboard

Setting the context

Old Mother Hubbard went to the cupboard to make herself a meal. She found that for once the cupboard wasn't bare. In it was... (the children add food items to the paper plates according to the pictures you have, which could include half a loaf of brown bread, a small amount of butter, chicken, chocolate biscuits, milk, fruit juice, water, an apple, a banana, cream, fish, tomatoes, lettuce, cheese and cake – see 'You will need').

The problem

How can we help her make a meal that is healthy and provides her with the nourishment she needs?

© Peter Rowe

Objectives

To learn that humans need **food** and water to stay alive.
To understand that there are many different kinds of foods.
To find out that eating the right types and amounts of food helps humans to keep **healthy**.

You will need

Photocopiable page 20 (alternatively, provide pictures of food from magazines); paper plates; scissors; glue; paper; pens.

Preparation

Cut enough pictures from magazines to give each group a set.

Discussion and research

- Talk to the children about foods that are definitely healthy and those that we should only eat a little of.
- Ask the children what they need to decide first before making a suitable meal for Old Mother Hubbard. *Which foods and drinks are healthier than others?*
- Take five minutes to look at the pictures of foods and drinks and to decide which ones are healthier than others.
- Talk about how to do this.

Obtaining evidence

- Working in groups, the children should then list all the foods and **fluids,** in their pictures, that are definitely healthy and those that are less healthy.
- Ask each group to agree and then choose the foods and drinks to make up one plate for Mother Hubbard's lunch that day.

Drawing together

- Look at the range of meals produced from the items in the cupboard.
- Decide whether there are enough for Old Mother Hubbard to have a varied diet over two and then three days. *What else does Mother Hubbard need to buy?*
- Write a shopping list for Mother Hubbard to replenish her stocks and to add extra foods and drinks that are healthy.

Support

Help the children to sort the foods and drinks into healthy and less healthy and explain that they should use only the healthy ones to make up a meal for Mother Hubbard's lunch.

Extension

Ask pairs of children to use their knowledge of healthy foods and drinks to make up a menu for one day for Mother Hubbard to follow. Ask them to share the menus and to write a shopping list of the healthy foods and drinks they are advising her to buy.

Scientific language

food – what we need to help us grow and stay alive.
fluids – liquids we can drink.
healthy – helping the body to stay fit and active.

Animal hide-and-seek

Setting the context

Rabbit got up early every morning so that he could have a good breakfast of lettuce leaves and carrots, before the people who owned the garden were up and about. After that, he went to spend the day with his friend, Grasshopper. Grasshopper liked to play hide-and-seek on most days because he always managed to find Rabbit and, he found such good places to hide himself, that he always had time for a nap! Rabbit had never found Grasshopper and had no idea where his friend hid each time. He was desperate to win the game of animal hide-and-seek by finding his friend and then finding a really good place to hide himself so that Grasshopper couldn't find him.

The problem

How can we help Rabbit decide where Grasshopper may be hiding? How can we help Rabbit find a really good place to hide?

Objectives

To be able to group animals according to their observable **features**.
To learn to decide how to find answers to questions.
To know how to make simple comparisons and identify simple patterns.

You will need

Pictures of a rabbit, grasshopper and other animals (birds, fish, worms, insects, reptiles, wild and domestic animals), and of different **habitats** set up on the computer or interactive screen and printed out for the children to use in the group activity.

Preparation

Take or find photographs on the internet (copyright permitting) of the different places in the school grounds, the local area and a contrasting area where animals may be found. Include pictures of a grassy area, wood, beach, meadow, vegetable garden, hedge, rainforest, pond, river and sea. Find pictures of a grasshopper, rabbit and other animals in the local and a contrasting area. Load these into your computer (copyright permitting) to display on a white screen.

Discussion and research

- Tell the children the story of Rabbit and Grasshopper and set up the first question.

- Ask the children for suggestions, and then ask them to talk to a partner to discuss the grasshopper's features, including its size, shape and colouring. *Will he fit inside the space available? Will he blend into the background?*
- Look at the photos of each habitat in turn and decide together where Grasshopper is most likely to hide if his friend can never find him. Ask the children to give reasons for their suggestions, focusing on the way he blends into the background but also the fact that he would survive in that particular habitat.

Obtaining evidence

- Ask the children to work in groups to answer the second question.
- Ask them to compare the features of Rabbit to each habitat and decide which ones would be good places for him to hide and which ones would not. They will need to consider whether he would survive, whether the habitat would be available in the local environment, and whether he would blend in.

Drawing together

- Discuss each habitat in turn and decide together which ones would be most suitable for Rabbit's hiding places.
- Talk about how animals need to blend into their backgrounds to keep themselves safe from predators.
- Look at the pictures of other animals and decide together which would be good places to hide for each one if they were playing a game of hide-and-seek with their friends or keeping themselves safe from predators.

Support

Play hide-and-seek with a group of children so that they can work out the need to make themselves small enough to fit inside a space, find a place that provides good cover and is of the same colour as the clothes they are wearing. Relate this to Rabbit's size, shape and colouring to find suitable places for him to hide.

Extension

Ask the children to sort the animals according to whether they are found in only one or more habitats. Ask them why rabbits can be found in several while sharks are only found in one. Challenge them to find one habitat suitable for more than one animal to use as a hiding place.

Scientific language

features – the parts of the body that make an animal look different to others; shapes, colours and patterns on an animal's coat.
habitat – a place where animals live that is natural to them and helps them survive and be comfortable.

Bird table

Setting the context

Mrs Twitcher has taken up bird watching as a new hobby. She has bought a bird table for her garden but she doesn't know what food she needs to put on it. Can you help her to find out what type of food will attract the most birds to her garden?

The problem

What type of food will attract the most birds to Mrs Twitcher's garden?

Objectives

To understand that animals need food and water to stay alive.
To be able to recognise when a test is unfair.
To know how to compare what happened with what they expected to happen and to try to explain it, drawing on their knowledge and understanding.

You will need

Three different types of bird food that are easily distinguishable from each other (most pet shops will sell lighter and darker brands, and peanuts); bird-feeders or shallow containers such as small yoghurt pots for the food; scales for measuring how much food is in each dish.

Preparation

Children will need to know the life processes common to all living things – they move, feed, grow and reproduce. They should have had the chance to relate these life processes to a variety of different animals, including themselves. This activity will need access to a bird-feeding area of some type. This does not need to be a bird table; the activity can be undertaken as easily by putting food in small containers on a normal table outside the classroom window. Make sure these are brought in at the end of the day to avoid attracting vermin. Obviously, a quieter area will be better when encouraging birds to feed. You may wish to screen off some windows with paper or make a 'hide' with holes cut for the children to observe birds feeding. Carry out this activity in winter and stop as soon as spring babies appear because birds need a balanced diet too and small birds need to learn to find their own food in the wild. This investigation will not take long to set up but will vary in length depending on how many birds feed at the table. It is wise to try this out in advance to make sure that birds will come to feed. If you find that other animals, such as squirrels, also visit the table, monitor this carefully. Rats are less welcome! This can be part of an ongoing activity for the class, focusing on caring for living things.

Discussion and research

- Introduce the problem.
- Give the children dishes of bird food to look at in groups, in a whole-class setting. They should use their senses to describe the food.
- Ask them to predict which food they think the birds will eat most.
- Hold a mini review to gather and record the children's ideas, asking them to explain their predictions.
- The children will need to identify how to make the test **fair**. If they are changing the type of food, they will need to keep everything else the same. It is particularly important to make sure that the children put out the same amount of food in each dish. They will also need to consider keeping the type, size and location of the dish the same.

They can make sure that the **quantity** of food is the same by weighing or filling identical containers to the same level. They will need to establish that they need to reweigh the dishes or compare the amount the level has gone down after a period of time to see how much food has been taken.

© Stockxchng

Obtaining evidence

- Once set up, the investigation will be fairly low maintenance, requiring small groups of children in turn to observe the table for 15-minute sessions over a day and then a week. They should use a tally chart to tally which of the three dishes each bird visits during their observation time. They could also try to identify the different types of bird that visit the table.
- When a reasonable quantity of food has been taken (this will be at your discretion), the children should weigh each dish or measure the change in levels to determine which has least food left. They can then think about how their findings relate to their predictions.

Drawing together

- Compare the results to see if one particular type of bird food is eaten most on every occasion or whether this changes over the week.
- The reporting back can be related to each set of findings. However, it is probably more useful to focus on whether the children's predictions match their findings. This can lead to a discussion of 'if not, why not?' Use questions such as: *Did you find out what you expected to? Why do you think this is?*
- It may be that the children identify that their initial prediction was flawed. Alternatively, they may establish that their investigation was flawed. Either way, it will be a valuable learning experience. Use questions such as: *What might you do differently if you did it again? Why would you do this?*

Support

Work closely with the children, questioning them as to why you are putting out the same amount of food, using identical containers and putting them in the same place. Ask an additional adult or a more confident child to help them tally the visits in the correct place. Do not expect them to notice the type of bird at this stage.

Extension

Ask the children to weigh the food to make sure the same amount is put out each time. Ask them to draw **conclusions** about whether there is a link between the type of food eaten most on each day and the type of bird visiting the table.

Scientific language

quantity – amount of (food).
conclusions – decisions based on evidence.
fair test – make everything except one thing equal or the same.

Mother Hubbard's bare cupboard

- Cut out the pictures below. Sort them as 'healthy' or 'less healthy'.
- Make a meal for Mother Hubbard. Stick some of the pictures onto her plate.

Chapter Two

Green plants and the environment

The six lessons in this chapter focus on plants and seeds and the conditions that they require for survival and growth.

The twins, Mike and Mary, who feature throughout this book, are introduced for the first time in **How do plants drink?** This lesson emphasises the importance of water for plants and the experiment shows that, with the use of dye, we can actually observe water being taken up by plants and spreading into leaves and flowers. It also introduces the vocabulary for different plant parts, reinforced in subsequent lessons throughout the chapter.

Through the creation of miniature 'greenhouses', **Creating a plant jungle** helps the children to understand more about the conditions that are required for plant life to survive (nutrients, light, warmth and water) and gives them an opportunity to see plants growing from seeds.

Take a closer look! demonstrates the variety that can be observed within a single species of plant. The activity allows children to closely examine a selection of clover leaves from different locations and present their findings in the form of drawings.

Jack's beans builds on the knowledge that children have acquired in earlier lessons, by showing what happens to plants when the conditions necessary for their survival are not present. Plants are deliberately deprived of soil, water and light, while children observe and record the results in an on-going whole-class activity.

The next lesson, **Seeds**, gives children the opportunity to examine seeds closely and to identify which plants grow from which seeds. This reinforces the idea that the same type of seed will always produce the same type of plant.

Eating plants focuses on the role of plants in our diet. The children will identify edible parts of plants e.g. roots, leaves. They will learn more about the nature of different fruits and vegetables as well as healthy eating.

How do plants drink?

Setting the context

Mike and Mary are staying at their grandma's house. While they are having their breakfast, she carries one of her favourite plants towards the sink and says, 'I'm just going to give it a drink of water.' The twins find this funny because they know plants can't drink like they do, but their grandma says, 'I can show you how plants have a drink – just come with me...'

The problem

Can you actually see plants 'drinking'?

Objectives

To know how to conduct a 'fair' experiment, observe closely what is happening and keep appropriate records.
To learn that plants need water to stay healthy.
To understand what plants require in order to grow and stay healthy.

You will need

Three white carnations and a stick of celery for each group; five containers to hold water for the plants; red and blue food colouring; a copy of photocopiable page 34 for each group.

Preparation

It will be useful if the children know what happens if plants are not watered. Grow some cress on the window sill and water some containers and not the others. Make sure there is space on the same windowsill for all the containers that will hold the carnations. Mix up the food colouring with water. Make sure you have enough for each container.

Discussion and research

- Tell the children about Mike and Mary's grandma giving her favourite plant a drink.
- Talk about the cress that has been watered and the differences they can see in the cress that has not had any water.
- Talk about how they think plants 'drink' water and where they get it from.
- Make sure that they understand that plants take in the water (sucked in through their **roots**) and that this water goes right

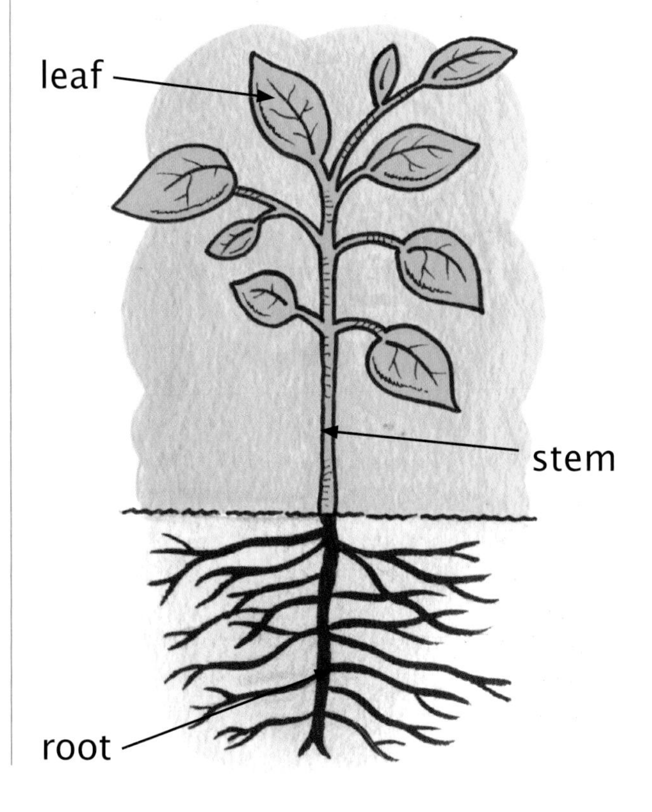

into the plant's leaves and **stem** and even into parts of the **flower**.

Obtaining evidence

- Give each group a copy of photocopiable page 34 and tell them that they are going to do an experiment to prove that plants draw up water.
- Explain that each of their containers will have coloured water. One carnation will be in blue water, one will be in red water, and one will have a split stem and be in both blue and red water. The celery will be in blue water.
- Talk to them about fair tests. Ask them what would make the test unfair. Try to make sure they understand about such things as the same amount of water in each container, the same stem lengths, putting the containers on the same windowsill, etc.
- Give three carnations, one of which has a split stem, and a stick of celery to each group. Make sure each stick of celery is the same length.
- Ask them to look at the celery. What do they see in the cut end? They should see the capillary tubes. What do they think they are for?
- Put each plant in a separate container and put them where the children can see what is happening.
- Ask them what they think will happen and record this on their sheets.

Drawing together

- During the day, the plants will draw up the coloured water in a spectacular way. The petals of the carnations should take in some of the coloured water. Let the children look at the cut end of the celery. They will be able to see the blue dye in the capillary tubes.
- Talk about what has happened, making sure that they understand that this process starts, in the plants' roots, which grow underground.

- Ask them to record what they saw and to colour in each of their drawings on the photocopiable page.

Further ideas

This experiment works with carnations. Will it work with other common flowers, such as dandelions, clovers and daffodils?

Photos © Peter Rowe

Support

Some children will need help in recording on the sheets and it will be useful to revise the simple parts of plants (roots, stems, etc.) with the whole class.

Extension

Give some children a simple drawing of a complete plant to label in detail. Some may even be capable of understanding some of the more complicated names for parts of the flower.

Scientific language

stem – the main part of the plant above the ground that supports the leaf, flower and fruit. Another name is 'stalk'.
flower – part of the plant from which fruit or seeds are later developed.
root.
roots - part of the plant found underground ground .

Creating a plant jungle

© Stockxchng

Setting the context

The twins, Mike and Mary, have been reading books and watching television programmes about jungles. They are fascinated by all the plants and trees that grow there and how different it is from their garden. 'I wish we lived in the jungle,' Mary said to her mum. 'Well,' mum said, 'I don't think we can do that but we can try to make one'. 'That's impossible,' said Mike. What do *you* think – is it possible?

The problem

How can we create a jungle effect in the classroom using readily available materials?

Objectives

To learn to turn ideas into a form that can be tested.
To be able to make and record observations.
To know how to use drawings to present results.

You will need

Large plastic sweet jars; warm, flat surface close to windows and lots of light; peat-free compost; plastic spray for water; magnifying glasses; seeds of small plants such as cress, little gem lettuces or night-scented stocks; some donated small house plants (preferably ones that flower); runner bean seeds; a copy of photocopiable page 35 for each group.

Preparation

The children will need some background knowledge through discussion, TV programmes, computer simulations or DVDs of jungles. They will also need to discuss what plants need for **growth** (light, water, warmth, soil or equivalent).

Discussion and research

- Ask the children about why plants are grown in greenhouses in this country in the winter. They should be able to tell you that the main reason is warmth.
- Ask them how they might make mini-greenhouses in the classroom.
- Show them the plastic sweet jars and talk about whether they think they can make a mini-greenhouse for Mike and Mary.

Obtaining evidence

- Organise the children into small groups and give each group a plastic sweet jar. Tell them that the jungle they make for Mike and Mary will be in the sweet jar, which will be lying on its side.
- Ask them what they will need next. They should mention **plants**, **seeds**, soil, water, etc.
- Give each group access to compost, seeds and plants and talk about how to plant the seeds and the plants so that they will grow.
- Show them the water sprays which will only be needed on the first day and then only if the compost dries out.
- Allow each group to make its jungle and place each sweet jar on a flat surface where it is warm and light.
- Give each group a copy of photocopiable page 35 and explain what they need to do.

Drawing together

- It is important that the children check their jungles each day and spray them with water if necessary.
- Each week, they will need to observe the jungles closely and complete their photocopiable pages.
- Magnifying glasses will be useful as the seeds start to grow.
- The plants should begin to fill the sweet jars and the runner beans will grow quickly and spread all over.
- Talk to the children about what is happening, why the plants are growing quickly and whether they think that their sweet jar is good enough to show to Mike and Mary.

Further ideas

There are all kinds of interesting experiments with plants, for example, watching a broad bean seed **germinate** or comparing plants grown under glass/polythene with those grown outside. There are all kinds of plants to grow and most children will enjoy growing food to eat, such as salad leaves that can be cut in the classroom and used in homemade sandwiches. Jungles can also be the inspiration for art lessons and huge wall displays can be made.

Support

The more adults that are available in the classroom when the children start filling and planting their sweet jars the better. Some children will also need support when they are writing about what they can see.

Extension

Some children might be interested in trying to understand why their greenhouses stay damp and why **condensation** forms on the inside of the sweet jar. They could also think about why some plants grow more quickly than others. There are jungles in many parts of the world. The children might be interested to see where they are on a world map. There are also important conservation issues related to trees (the Amazon, for example) that some children might be capable of understanding.

Scientific language

growth – an increase in size.
seed – small part that grows into a plant of the same kind.
germination – the sprouting of a plant.
condensation – the process of steam turning to water on a cold surface.
plant – a living organism usually with roots and leaves.

Take a closer look!

Setting the context

Mike and Mary were bored. They had been looking for a four-leafed clover and hadn't found one. When they were back in their classroom, they were surprised when their teacher said, 'I agree with you. If you don't find a four-leafed clover it can be boring, but there's more to clovers than having four leaves, you know. Even the ones with three leaves are really interesting, if you look closely enough'. Well, the twins didn't believe her. Do you?

The problem

What is interesting about clover leaves? Can we find out by looking at some clover leaves from the school field?

Objectives

To learn to find differences in plants in the immediate environment.
To be able to make and record observations.
To know how to use drawings to present results.

You will need

Lots of clover leaves from different parts of the school field; magnifying glasses; crayons and pencils (not felt-tipped pens); paper; wide sticky tape; sticky labels (optional); polythene bags; a copy of photocopiable page 36 for each child.

Preparation

Take the children outside to look at different leaves on bushes, trees and flowers. Ask them to look carefully at them using the magnifying glasses and to describe what they see. They could also draw some of their favourite leaves. Take a collection into the classroom and talk about the **veins** and the different shapes. Ask the children how they could **classify** them – by shape, number of points, etc.

Discussion and research

- Ask the children whether they think clover leaves are interesting, like Mike and Mary's teacher, or whether they agree with the twins that they are boring. Find out why.
- Divide them into small groups and give each group four clover leaves from different plants. Ask them to use their magnifying glasses to look at the patterns on each leaf.
- There will be considerable differences. Ask them to describe the shapes and the patterns and to choose one to draw.
- These can either be closely observed scientific drawings or huge works of art for wall displays.

Obtaining evidence

© Stockxchng

- Give each child a copy of photocopiable page 36 and take them on to the school field in their small groups.
- Ask them to choose four different places where clover is growing and to write a name for each place on their sheet. Descriptions such as: near to the gate, by the sand pit, near to the tree, etc. are all suitable.
- Each group will need to pick ten different leaves at random from each place and put them in their plastic bags with a label showing which part of the field they are from.
- Back in the classroom, they need to start sorting each of the bags into **groups** using the different patterns on the clover leaves.

Drawing together

- Every single clover leaf might have a different pattern, or there might be only two or three different patterns. There might be common patterns across all four different places or each place might have very distinct and different patterns.
- They will need to choose interesting samples from each place or the ones that are the most common to draw on their photocopiable pages. It is best to do this using a magnifying glass.
- Samples of the real leaves can be pressed and mounted as a display.
- As you are doing this, it is important to discuss whether they think they could tell the twins that clover leaves are interesting!

Further ideas

The whole of the clover plant from its roots through to its flowers could be studied. It is an important plant for bees and as a source of green manure for farmers. This can lead to more work on bees, fertilisation, etc. The patterns on the leaves can also make fascinating patterns for art as paintings and collages.

Support

Collecting the leaves and being accurate about putting them in the correct bags and labelling them correctly can be difficult, as can using sticky tape to mount the leaves. It is important to have as many adults, to help in the classroom, as possible.

Extension

There can be lots of different patterns on the leaves and some children will want to try and identify them all. Are the patterns on the leaves of white or red clover different or similar?

Scientific language

classify – sorting items into scientific categories.
grouping – sorting items into groups.
veins – part of a leaf's structure

Jack's beans

Setting the context

Laura got to thinking when her teacher was reading the story of *Jack and the Beanstalk*. Jack was given five beans and yet only one grew to be strong enough for Jack to climb. Why did one grow taller and stronger than the others, and why didn't the others grow so strong and tall?

The problem

How can we help Laura to find out if and why some plants grow taller and stronger than others?

Objectives

To understand that plants need light and water to grow.
To be able to recognise and name the leaf, flower, stem and root of a flowering plant.
To learn that seeds grow into flowering plants.

You will need

Bean seeds; grow bag; water; string; canes; flower pots; cotton wool; digital camera; tally charts on photocopiable pages 37 and 38 for each of the beans to record the number of days it takes for each of the beans to start to shoot.

Preparation

Clear a space in front of a window and set up the grow bag, canes and string for the beans to climb as they grow. Find a dark place such as a cupboard. Set up a display for a picture diary of each bean's growth. Prepare an area outside to transplant the beans to. The best time for this activity is at the start of the summer term.

Discussion and research

- Collect the children's ideas on why they think one of Jack's beans grew stronger than the others. If they were magic beans, why did only one grow to be so tall and strong?

- Identify with the children what seeds need to grow. They will probably come up with **soil** because it gives food or **nutrients**, water and light. Explain that all plants need food, water and light to stay alive.
- Set up as fair a test as you can to try out the children's ideas. Plant five beans in the grow bag in front of the window, explaining that the beans will all have food from the soil, light from the window and will be watered every day.
- Take a digital photograph and start off the picture diary of the beans' growth.
- Plant another bean in cotton wool and place it by the side of those in the grow bag, explaining that you are trying to grow this one without soil. Plant another in a pot and put this one by the grow bag, explaining that this one will not have water once it starts to grow. Plant another in a pot and put this in a dark place, explaining that this one will be watered but will not get any light.
- Take a photo of each bean to start its picture diary and set up a tally chart for each of these beans.

Obtaining evidence

- Look after the beans in the grow bag, cotton wool and dark place.
- Stop watering the bean, in the pot next to the grow bag, as soon as it starts to shoot.
- Every day, check each bean with the children, and make a tally on each chart to record the number of days it takes for each stage to be reached.
- Take a photo of each bean as soon as it shoots, labelling the picture with the correct number of days and adding it to the bean diary.
- Take pictures every day and note when the **leaves** and **flowers** appear. You may need to transplant the beans outside before the flowers appear.
- Encourage the children to recognise and name each part of the plant as it grows and label these on the photos.

Drawing together

- A week after the beans have started to grow **stems**, or in time to prevent the bean from dying, look at the bean that has not been watered and note that it has started to die. *What can we deduce from this?* (That plants need water to grow.) Give the bean plant a good drink to revive it if you can.
- Next, look at the bean in the dark place and compare it with those which have had light. You may need to do this over a few days, but as soon as the children notice the differences with the ones that have had light, take a photo for the bean diary and put it in the light so it can also revive itself. Ask the children, *Why does the plant grow so long and thin? What is it looking for?* Explain that plants need light to help them make a special food which helps them grow into healthy plants.
- Next, look at the one grown on cotton wool. *Has this bean managed to grow? Is it as strong and tall as those in the grow bag?*
- Add the children's observations and comments to the bean diaries.

Support

Talk to the children, in a small group, asking them direct questions that require them to look at specific parts of the plant.

Extension

Ask some children to use books and Internet websites to find out why plants need light to grow.

Scientific language

stem – the main part of the plant above the ground that supports the leaf, flower and fruit. Another name is 'stalk'.
leaf – part of the plant that grows from the side of the stem, branch or root.
flower – part of the plant from which fruit or seeds are later developed.
soil – earth in which plants grow.
nutrients – sources of nourishment.

Seeds

Setting the context

Mr Handy got up early one morning and looked through his window. The sun was shining, so he could go out into his garden and plant his seeds. Now, where did he put them last year? Oh yes, he had put the packets of seeds into a paper bag inside a drawer in his cupboard in the garage. When he had finished his breakfast, he went outside to find his tools and seeds. When he opened the bag, he was very annoyed. All the seeds had come out of their packets and got all mixed up. How on earth was he going to separate them so that the same kind of seeds were together? How could he find out what each seed would grow into so that he could label them once they were planted?

The problem

How can we help Mr Handy separate his seeds? How can we help him find out which plant each variety of seeds will grow so that he can label them correctly?

Objectives

To be able to group **seeds** according to their similarities and differences.
To find out about different seeds and plants.
To understand that **flowering plants** produce seeds of the same kind.

You will need

A collection of flower and vegetable seeds that are very different in size, shape and colour, such as sunflower, marrow, carrot, peas, beans, lettuce and orange pips; sieves with holes of different thicknesses; empty seed packets that match the seeds in your collection; card and pens to write labels; reference sheet of seeds and names in your collections.

Preparation

It would be useful if the children have had some experience of growing seeds, such as the **Jack's beans** activity in this chapter. Make sure you choose seeds that have not been treated and are safe for the children to handle. Include some seeds that the children will not recognise easily. Make six sets of mixed-up seeds. Use different seeds for each group if you can. Leave a few seeds inside each seed packet for the children to compare with the ones in their sets and make a reference sheet to use during the group activity if the children get stuck or mix up the remaining seeds. Use photocopiable page 39 if desired.

Discussion and research

- Sit the children in a circle and pass enough sunflower seeds around to ensure one between two children. Ask the children to talk to a partner about the colour, size and shape of the seeds. Discuss the seeds' similarities and differences. Agree that the seeds all belong to the same plant and that when planted will grow into the same flowering plant. If no one can say what that is, tell them that the seeds should grow into sunflowers with the right **conditions** and if looked after properly.
- Identify the conditions the seeds will need to grow.
- Look at the seeds in your first set. Which ones do the children recognise? They will probably recognise the bean and pea seeds.
- How can we find out what plants the other seeds will grow into? What sources can we use? The children may suggest using

reference materials or looking at the empty packets to see if there is a stray seed left inside.
- Invite them to talk with a partner to think of a way of helping Mr Handy separate the seeds. Collect a small number of ideas for the whole class to listen to.

© Peter Rowe

Obtaining evidence
- Organise the children into groups and ask them to find a way of separating the seeds in their set. Ask them to put each different variety onto a separate sheet of paper. When they have done this, ask them to come up with a way of finding out which plant each seed will grow into. They will need to be very careful not to lose the stray seeds out of the empty packets if they use these as reference materials.
- If the children get stuck, tell the children the next part of the story. *Mr Handy decided it was time for a cup of tea. As he was sipping his favourite brew, he remembered that he had kept a list of all the seeds he had in his collection. Now, what did he do with it and did it have the seeds on as well as the name?* Produce your sheet of seeds and names at this point. Ask the children to use it to compare their seeds with the ones on the list and to find the names.
- Ask them to write labels for each variety of seed in their set.
- Invite half of the children in each group to go around each table in turn to look at the seeds and labels. The other half should remain seated to explain how they separated the seeds and found the correct names. Make sure the children are moving on after half a minute at the most. Swap over.

Drawing together
List all the different seeds that are in the whole collection. Agree that each seed will grow into a flowering plant. Talk about the conditions they will need. Decide whether you have helped Mr Handy separate his seeds and helped him to label each one correctly.

Support
Give the children seeds that are very different in size, shape and colour. Include the sunflower and bean seeds to give them a head start.

Extension
Give some of the children a shorter target time in which to sort and label the seeds. While they do this, make sure the other groups are on task, sorting and labelling their seeds. Work with the more able group to talk about how the flowering plant produces seeds which then grow into more flowering plants of the same kind. Draw the life cycle of one of the seeds.

Scientific language
seed – small part that grows into a plant of the same kind.
flowering plant – a plant that grows flowers.
conditions for growth – what seeds need to help them grow into healthy plants.

Eating plants

Setting the context

Heidi needs to lose some weight and has been told about a fantastic new diet that helps her eat healthily but requires her to eat only two plant parts each day. She knows that nearly every plant has roots, stems, leaves, flowers and seeds but she is not very good at knowing which part of the plant is which and she is unsure how to find out.

The problem

How can we help Heidi find out which part of the plant she can eat?

© Peter Rowe

Objectives

To be able to recognise and name the **leaf**, **stem**, **root** and **flower** of flowering plants.
To know how to group plants according to their similarities and differences.

You will need

Sorting rings; a collection of **fruits** and **vegetables**, including a potato; labels for stem, leaf, root, flower, seed and fruit; sheets of paper labelled with the parts that we eat; a copy of photocopiable page 40; reference materials.

Preparation

Make sure the fruits and vegetables are clean and safe to handle. Be careful with vegetables such as the potato. This vegetable is part of the stem even though it seems to grow from the root system. Later, in 'Drawing together', you may like to draw the children's attention to the fact that potatoes go green when left in the light because the sun helps plants make a special food, a chemical called chlorophyll, to help them grow. That is why the leaves and stems of some plants also turn green, when left in the light. You may wish to explain that we do not eat potatoes, after they have turned green, as this may not be safe.

Discussion and research

- Sit the children as a class, in a circle, with the collection of fruit and vegetables in the centre. Choose one fruit or vegetable and describe the features, and name each one.
- Ask the children to say which one is their favourite one to eat and why.
- Then ask them: *Which part of the plant is it? Which part of this plant do we eat?*
- Put two sorting rings in the centre of the circle and label one 'root' and the other 'leaf'. Explain that the labels refer to the part of the fruit or vegetable that we eat.
- Choose a carrot and talk about which part of the vegetable we eat. Put it in the set labelled 'root'.
- Now decide whether the lettuce goes in the set labelled 'root' or 'leaf'.
- Repeat this for two more vegetables.
- Ask the children to find more plants of which we eat the root or leaf.

Obtaining evidence

- Give each group a collection of fruit and

leaf

root

© Peter Rowe

vegetables and ask them to sort them into sets according to the part that we eat, by putting them onto the matching sheet of paper.

- Complete photocopiable page 40 to consolidate the children's learning.

Drawing together

- Look at other fruits and vegetables that the children have not sorted so far and decide together in which set they belong.
- Choose two of the children's sets and write a menu for Heidi to enjoy a nutritious and delicious breakfast, lunch and dinner.

Support

Ask a supporting adult to work with some of the children in order to sort the vegetables into roots and leaves. They could also make a vegetable soup which could be shared with the rest of the class.

Extension

Include fruits and vegetables from abroad such as pumpkin, sweet potato and ginger, and things that animals eat such as acorns, ash and sycamore keys and seeds. Use the internet or reference books to help the children find out the answers if they are unsure.

Scientific language

fruit – a container that holds seeds.
seed – small part that grows into a plant of the same kind.
vegetable – a plant grown for food.
root – part of the plant normally below the ground that helps the plant anchor itself or keep itself in place and takes nourishment or food from the soil to other parts of the plant.
stem – main part of the plant above the ground that supports the leaf, flower and fruit. Another name is 'stalk'.
leaf – part of the plant that grows from the side of the stem, branch or root.
flower – part of the plant from which fruit or seeds are later developed.

How do plants drink ?

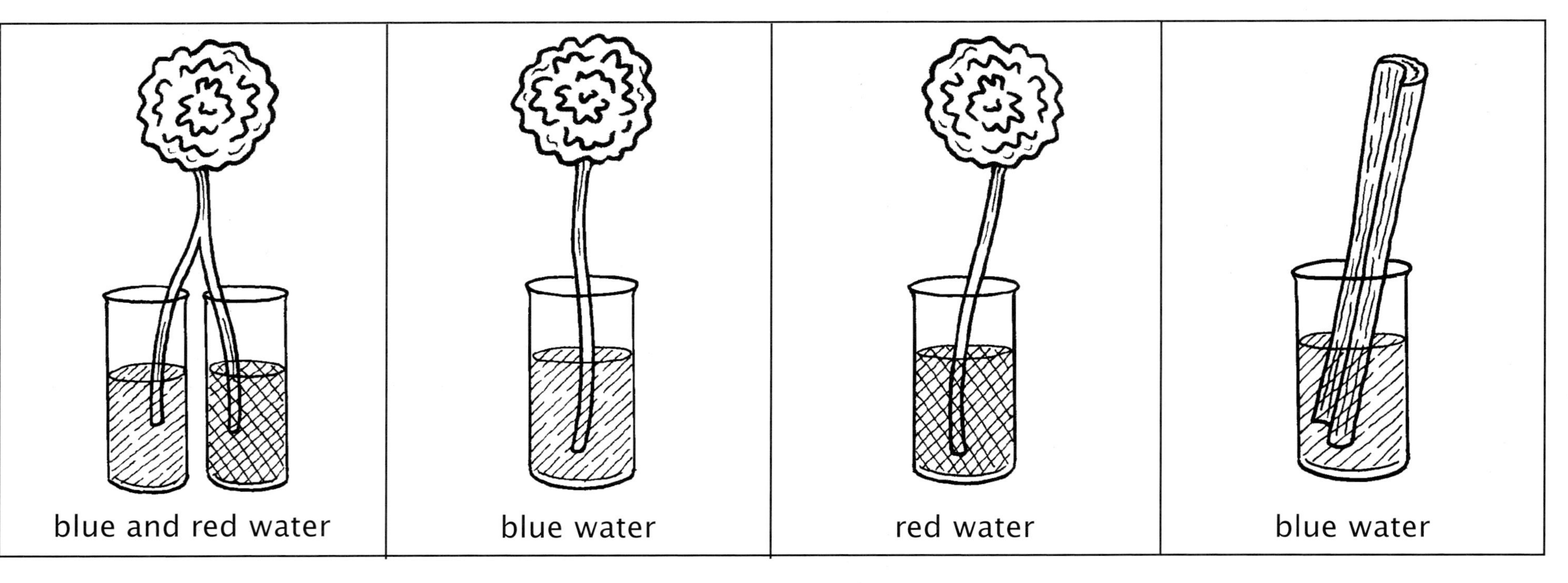

What do I think might happen?	What did I do to make it a fair test?
What do I see happening?	Colour in the pictures to show what happened.

Creating a plant jungle

- Look at your sweet jar jungle each week. Draw and write what you see.

Week 1 Draw your jungle	**Week 2** Draw your jungle
Write what is happening	Write what is happening
Week 3 Draw your jungle	**Week 4** Draw your jungle
Write what is happening	Write what is happening

Take a closer look!

Where? ____________________ ____________________	Where? ____________________ ____________________
Where? ____________________ ____________________	Where? ____________________ ____________________

Jack's beans

- Tally the number of days it takes for each shoot to appear and grow leaves, flowers and beans.

	Bean 1	**Bean 2**	**Bean 3**	**Bean 4**	**Bean 5**
Shoot					
Leaves					
Flowers					
Beans					

Jack's beans 2

- Tally the number of days it takes for each bean to appear and grow leaves, flowers and beans.

	Bean in cotton wool	**Bean without water**	**Bean in dark place**
Shoot			
Leaves			
Flowers			
Beans			

Seeds

marrow

lettuce

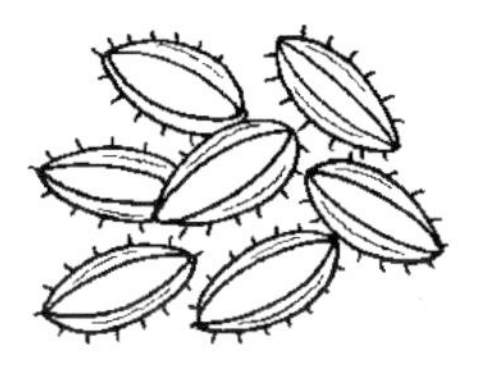

carrot

sunflower

orange

broad bean

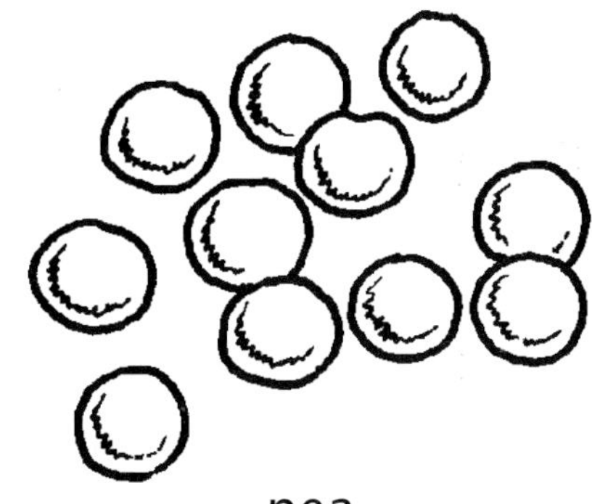

pea

Eating plants

- Match each fruit and vegetable to the plant part that we eat:

lettuce
carrot
tomato
apple
cabbage
broccoli
celery
parsnip

flower
root
seed
fruit
stem
leaf

- Add two fruits or vegetables of your own.

Chapter Three

Forces and motion

This chapter contains six experiments which are designed to show the effects of gravity, air resistance and friction, and the ways in which objects can be moved by pulling or pushing. The activities marked with an asterisk * explore particularly challenging concepts and should be used as enrichment lessons, to stretch more confident learners, if appropriate.

Getting the balance right introduces the concepts of gravity, centre of gravity and balancing, through an activity based around the construction of a balancing mobile.
The world's best parachute* reinforces the children's knowledge of gravity and also teaches them about floating and air resistance. The children construct and test a range of model parachutes to find out which types work best and why.

Hungry Ivor encourages children to think about the ways objects can be made to move and, in particular, the idea of movement being caused by pulling. The lesson poses a puzzle which can be solved by constructing a simple pulley.

In **Whose car goes the furthest?** children experiment with toy cars and ramps. This not only adds to their existing knowledge about how to make objects move, but also gives them additional opportunities to understand how to design and carry out a fair test.

In **The lorries and the steep hill*** another experiment, using ramps, demonstrates the effects of friction. The lesson also encourages children to think about different situations in which friction can occur.

The marble race shows how pushing can make objects move, change pace or direction. The children design a game which uses a pushing force to control the movement of marbles.

Getting the balance right

Setting the context

Mike and Mary's uncle, Will Daubalot, the famous artist, is having problems. He has been trying to make a mobile to hang in his new art gallery but he can't seem to get it to balance. He has drawn and painted all the beautiful shapes to hang on his mobile but it still won't work. He is very worried because the first visitors to his exhibition will be arriving in a few hours time. What do you think he can do? Can you help?

The problem

What is Will doing that is stopping the mobile from balancing? Can you help him make mobiles that balance and hang properly?

Objectives

To learn to observe, explore and ask questions.
To begin to understand what gravity, **centre of gravity** and **balance** mean.

You will need

Rulers; pencils or small pieces of dowel; Plasticine®; metal coat hangers straightened so the wire is approximately 40cm long (or similar gauge wire); thin card; cotton thread.

Preparation

The children need to begin to understand what 'balance' means and how they can make something balance by finding its centre (of gravity) and by placing objects in different positions along its length.

Discussion and research

- The children should be in small groups with as much adult support as possible.
- Give each group a ruler, pencil or a short piece of dowel and ask them to balance the ruler on the pencil like a see-saw. Talk about what they have to do, such as making sure the centre of the ruler is balanced on the pencil.
- Give each group a small lump of Plasticine® and tell them to put pieces of Plasticine® on both ends of the ruler so that it still balances.
- Ask them what they have to do with the

Plasticine®. Talk about it having to be the same weight at each end, or if the weight is different, they can make it balance by putting the Plasticine® at different points on the ruler, not just at the ends.

- Now tell them to move the ruler so that it is not balanced in the centre. *What do they have to do to balance the ruler this time?*

Obtaining evidence

- Tell the children that they are going to show Will Daubalot how to make a mobile that balances.
- Give each group a length of coat hanger wire, cotton and thin card.
- They need to make shapes to hang on the mobile. It might be better to use a theme, such as mathematical shapes, birds or butterflies. The shapes could be decorated or not, depending on how artistic you want the children to be.
- First of all, make shapes to hang at each end of the wire and then, if the children are skilful enough, they could make a cross-shaped mobile.
- The children will need constant support to help them 'balance' the mobile by hanging the shapes at the appropriate point on the wire and having the cotton to hang the mobile from in the right place.

Drawing together

- Hang up the finished mobiles.
- Discuss with the children why their mobiles balance – or why they don't!
- The forces **pulling** down at each end of the wire have to balance. They are '**balanced forces**' and the centre of gravity has to be in the right place so that the mobile hangs properly.
- Ask each group whether they think they have helped Will Daubalot. *Will he be pleased with their mobiles?*

Further ideas

The children could make see-saws that hold model people or design an outdoor playground with all kinds of play equipment that works using 'balance' of some kind. The mobiles could use 3D shapes.

Support

The more adults in the classroom the better, because the construction of the mobiles can be difficult for most children. 'Gravity', 'centre of gravity' and 'balanced forces' are difficult concepts but easy to see working. Some children will be able to use them but others will need to be helped to understand.

Extension

It should be possible for more confident learners to illustrate and describe, in a step by step way, what they are doing and why their mobile works.

Scientific language

balanced forces – when two opposing forces are equal.
pulling – moving an object towards oneself, or the source of the force.
balance – an even distribution of weight.
centre of gravity – balancing point.

The world's best parachute

Setting the context

Oscar Longdrop spends all his spare time jumping out of aeroplanes, opening his parachute and landing on the grass at summer fêtes. The crowds always love him and he gets lots of applause and cheers. Now he wants a better parachute. In fact, he wants one that will come down much more slowly so that all the excited crowds that watch him will be able to see him in the sky for longer. Can you help?

The problem

Can you make a parachute that will float through the air as slowly as possible? What material will you use and how will you test it?

Objectives

To learn to explore, observe and ask questions. To begin to understand **air resistance**, **pulling** and **gravity**.

You will need

30cm square pieces of thin material; cotton thread: scissors; masking tape; Plasticine®; a parachute that you (the teacher) have made that works; a copy of photocopiable page 54 for each pair.

Preparation

Talk to the children about what a parachute is and what it does. Ask them questions about falling to the ground and introduce the concepts of gravity, floating and air resistance. For example, *Why does a parachute float? What stops the parachutist from just falling? What does the parachute actually do?* Talk about the weight of the parachutist and the size of the parachute. *What would happen if the parachute was really too big? What would happen if it was too small?*

Discussion and research

- With the children in twos, give each pair a copy of photocopiable page 54 and show them your parachute.
- Take them outside and carefully throw your parachute in the air. Before you do this, make sure that it works! Repeat some of the earlier questions and ask: *Why is it **falling** down? Why is it falling slowly? What is stopping it from falling too quickly?*
- Talk through the two drawings on the photocopiable page and explain what they are going to do and that their parachute design will help Oscar Longdrop give an even better parachuting display.

Obtaining evidence

- The children need to cut out a circle from their pieces of material. The sizes will vary, which is fine, but make sure that they don't cut too small a circle.
- It is important to remind them that the

size of the 'canopy' of the parachute is very important.

Parachute © Peter Rowe Scenery © Stockxchng

- Using the picture on photocopiable page 54 as a guide, the children should attach four pieces of cotton to the material with tape. The loose ends of the cotton should then be attached to a small piece of Plasticine®.
- After they have attached their Plasticine® (don't forget that the weight has to be appropriate – not too heavy and not too light), the parachutes are ready to be tested.
- When you go outside, take more Plasticine® in a plastic container.
- Let each pair test their parachute and talk about why it did or did not work. You might find it easier to do the tests yourself. This might make a fairer test.

Drawing together

- If the parachutes float away – ask the children why – they will need more Plasticine®. If they fall too quickly, they will need less.
- Discuss why certain parachutes work better than others.
- Ask each pair to complete photocopiable page 54 and display the working parachutes around the classroom as Oscar Longdrop will be using their designs to help him thrill the crowds!

Further ideas

Air resistance can be a fascinating concept for children. One really simple way of showing them how powerful air resistance can be is to take them out into the playground, with very large pieces of card, on a windy day. Ask the children to hold their card so that it is facing the wind. They will be able to feel a very powerful force pushing against them. (This also reinforces why parachutes must have a large surface area.)

Support

The more adults in the classroom the better, because some children will need help cutting out their parachutes. Testing them will also be easier if there are adults to help each pair and to ask them questions about why their parachutes work (or don't work) and about the scientific concepts involved.

Extension

More confident children might want to experiment with different shapes of parachutes; for example, squares and rectangles; or parachutes with holes cut in them. Different materials could be used such as tissue paper or heavier cloth. Parachutes with more cotton attached might also encourage more ideas about how to make them work better.

Scientific language

air resistance – the force of the air against objects moving through it.
gravity – the force that pulls objects towards the Earth.
pulling – moving an object towards oneself, or the source of the force.
falling – dropping towards the ground.

Hungry Ivor

Setting the context

Ivor Lamp, the lighthouse keeper, needs your help. He can't get down the stairs to collect his lunch from the boat that brings his food or get to the kitchen to make himself a sandwich. This is because the stairs are being mended and it is far too dangerous to use them. In fact, he is stuck at the top. It's 12.30 and Ivor can see the boat coming. He's also very, very hungry. He really needs his lunch. What can he do? Can you help?

The problem

Can you design a machine that will lift Ivor's lunch from the boat and up to the top of the lighthouse? What will you need and how will you make it?

Objectives

To begin to understand that **pulling** things can make objects start moving.
To be able to make suggestions about how objects can be made to move and to find out whether they were right.
To gain experience of asking questions about what is causing movement.

You will need

Scrap paper; wire to make a triangular shape; cotton reels to thread on to the wire; string; Plasticine® or other materials to make Ivor Lamp's lunch; a device such as a hook to attach the wire triangle to the top of a bench or desk; other materials that the children might need to make their own designs.

Preparation

Tell the children the problem that the lighthouse keeper has and how he really does need his lunch. Make sure that this whole class discussion begins to identify the real problem, which is how to pull up his lunch from the bottom to the top from the outside because he cannot use the stairs. Use the whiteboard and scrap paper to draw, or get the children to draw, as many of their ideas as possible. As you are doing this, talk about each idea and whether they think it will work or not. Don't forget to ask them why.

Illustration © Garry Davis

Discussion and research

- Ask the children to work in pairs and to use scrap paper again to try and draw how they are going to help the lighthouse keeper.
- When they have reached a decision about what they are going to do, ask them to draw a neat version of how they will make sure the lighthouse keeper gets his lunch. They should also describe how to make it and suggest why they think it will work.

Obtaining evidence

- You now have to make a decision. If you have managed to talk to each pair of children and haved helped them to channel their discussions, they should all have thought of a simple **pulley**. Many of the children might be able to make what they have thought of with very little help from you. If this is the case, give them some suitable materials and let them do it.
- If you do not feel that this is the best way forward, each pair could make a simple pulley system based on the illustration above.

Drawing together

- You will need to ask each pair of children to demonstrate whether their 'machine' works. In other words, will Ivor Lamp get his lunch?
- Discuss why the pulleys work and what they need to work best. Some suggestions might include that the cotton reel needs to roll smoothly over the wire, the string needs to be strong enough, etc.

Further ideas

Why not make this much more real? Once all of the children have decided how they are going to get the lunch to Ivor, why not make a lighthouse during a design and technology lesson – complete with a light and with a pulley system fixed to it? (This activity is based on the story *The Lighthouse Keeper's Lunch* by Ronda and David Armitage, Scholastic Children's Books).

Support

Once again, in practical activities of this kind it is best to have as many adults in the classroom as possible. Some children will need support in writing explanations and if this is too difficult just allow them to draw what they are doing.

Extension

Pulleys and the **forces** involved can be much more complicated than just one cotton reel. Some children might like to answer the question: *How can you make a pulley that will* **lift** *quite heavy objects?*

Scientific language

force – power exerted on an object.
pull – to move an object towards oneself, or the source of the force.
lift – to move an object upwards.
pulley – a system of wheels and cords used to lift or move an object.
gravity – the force that pulls objects towards the Earth.

Whose car goes the furthest?

Setting the context

The twins, Mike and Mary, have each received a toy car for their birthday. They have been pushing them along the floor and letting them go. Both cars went quite a long way. Then Mike started boasting. 'My car will go much further than yours,' he said. 'No, it won't,' said Mary, 'mine will go much further than yours.' 'No, it won't,' Mike repeated, until eventually they started arguing and shouting at each other. They started to push the cars faster and harder but couldn't agree which of their cars would go the furthest. Can you help them stop arguing with each other?

The problem

How can we make both cars travel further to stop the twins from arguing?

Objectives

To be able to make suggestions about how objects can be made to move and to find out whether they were right.

To learn to explore, observe and ask questions.

To understand **fair tests** and how to record results.

You will need

Building blocks or books; a smooth plank of wood and a smooth floor surface; metre rulers; several toy cars (all as similar as possible); a copy of photocopiable page 55 for each child.

Preparation

You need to be able to build a ramp like the one in the drawing below. The children will need to be able to **measure** how far their car travels along the floor, using a metre ruler. It will be useful to practise measuring accurately beforehand.

Discussion and research

- Tell the whole class about Mike and Mary's argument and ask them for suggestions that will help them to make both of their cars travel further.
- Show the class the cars that you will be using later.
- Some of the suggestions will involve **pushing** the cars along so there will be opportunities to talk about **forces** and how objects are made to move.
- Ask whether they can make a **fair test** by pushing the cars.
- Draw some of their ideas on the whiteboard.
- Give each child a copy of photocopiable page 55 and ask them to draw either their

idea or the one they think is the best one so far.

Photos © Peter Rowe

Obtaining evidence

- They need to understand about fair tests and that each time the car has to be moved in exactly the same way.
- Discuss with them how to build a ramp and how it will be possible to make it at different heights, using blocks or books.
- Discuss how the car will be allowed to move down the ramp. Those who have understood what 'fair test' means will realise that they will just have to let the car go from exactly the same position and not push it at all.
- Give a car to each small group. The groups could either take turns to use one ramp or they could build their own ramps.
- Explain how important it is to complete the measurements accurately on the photocopiable page.

Drawing together

- Each group should be allowed to discuss their results with the class and to say when their car went the furthest.
- They should also be encouraged to demonstrate making the car travel the furthest distance and try to explain why.
- Ask the class whether Mike and Mary could use this method to stop them arguing.
- *How would they explain to them that it was a fair test?*
- Ask them to complete the final section on the photocopiable page.

Further ideas

See the next activity which uses the same ramp but looks at the forces that stop objects from moving.

Support

The children need to understand what a fair test is. Some children will need help with measuring how far the car travels. Others may prefer to measure using direct comparison, (marking the distance that each car travels). Check carefully that they are not pushing the cars down the ramp. Some children may need support in writing their explanation.

Extension

Ask the children what they think would happen if they used two cars and one had bigger wheels than the other. Try this out, using a similar chart to record what happens. Ask them why they think the car with the bigger wheels travelled further.

Scientific language

fair tests – tests in which everything is kept the same each time, expect the item that is being tested.
measurement – working out size using fixed units, such as cm.
force – power exerted on an object.
pushing – moving an object away from oneself, or the source of the force.

The lorries and the steep hill

Setting the context

Bessie Buildit, the engineer, was standing at the top of a steep hill on a very busy road. She had a problem. Sometimes when very heavy lorries were going down the hill, their brakes didn't work properly and they couldn't stop safely. She had been asked to try to make the hill safe for the lorries. So far she hasn't had any good ideas. Do you think you could help her?

The problem

How can you make the lorries stop safely and quickly, but not too suddenly (because that could hurt the driver)?

Objectives

To be able to choose a material for a specific purpose.

To learn to observe, ask questions and conduct a fair test.

To know how to make suggestions about how an object can be made to stop and to find out whether they are right.

You will need

The same ramps you used in **Whose car goes the furthest?**; the shiniest and smoothest floor surface in the school; metre rulers; a range of different toy lorries – as heavy as possible, but they must be able to fit on to the ramp properly; different materials such as corduroy, different grades of sandpaper, small sand tray, corrugated cardboard etc.; some shoes or trainers with different designs on the soles; a copy of photocopiable page 56 for each child.

Preparation

You will need to have the ramps set up and all the lorries available. For the first part of the activity, you also need to make available a range of different shoes or trainers with various designs on the soles.

Discussion and research

- The children will need to know that **friction** is a **force**.
- One of the easiest ways to demonstrate this is to start by looking at the soles of shoes and asking questions such as: *Why are the soles* **rough** *and patterned? What would happen if they were* **smooth** *and shiny? Is it easier to walk across a carpet or across ice and why?*
- It can also be linked to sport. *Why are goalkeepers' gloves rough and not smooth?* Or it can be linked to cars by asking why car tyres have patterns on them.

- Give each child a copy of photocopiable page 56 and ask them to complete the first part. It might be better to go through this with them as a whole class.
- When they have finished, talk about their answers and make sure that they understand what friction does.

Obtaining evidence

- Show the children the ramp, the lorries and the different materials and remind them how the ramp works when it is at a height of about 30cm.
- Talk to them about Bessie Buildit's problem.
- Tell them that she needs their help to test some of the materials.
- Ask them how they might do the tests.
- Where they place the material might be important e.g. will the material be better up against the end of the ramp or some distance away?
- Each small group should have a collection of materials and should write down which one they think will work best.
- They now need to do their tests and experiment with the different materials and where they put them on the slippery floor.
- Remind them that the lorry should not stop too quickly or the driver will be hurt, and that it should definitely not fall over.

Drawing together

- Ask each group to demonstrate which material they think works best and to explain where to place it on the floor.
- Talk about what advice they would give to Bessie.
- Ask them why some materials did not work at all.

Further ideas

Why not think of an experiment to find out which shoe sole pattern is the best for keeping its grip?

Support

Some children will need help with the whole idea of friction and may find completing the photocopiable page difficult without support. This activity needs a lot of discussion. It would be useful to have several adults working with the children.

Extension

The size of the lorry's wheels and the lorry's weight will make a difference to how it stops and is worth exploring with some children who will be interested in how this works in real life. Lorries do have escape lanes on some steep roads. There may be some illustrations, computer programs or broadcasts available that show this. *What are they made of and why? How do they work?*

Scientific language

force – power exerted on an object.
friction – the resistance, or 'sticking', that occurs when one object moves over another.
smooth – uneven, with no bumps.
rough – uneven and bumpy to touch.

The marble race

Setting the context

It is a rainy Sunday afternoon and Mike and Mary are bored and can't find anything to do. Mike had just finished his milkshake and was making irritating noises by blowing down the straw. Mary was rolling a marble backwards and forwards across the tabletop. Suddenly, they looked at each other, grinned and Mary said, 'I've got a great idea for a game.' What was the great idea?

The problem

What game can you help the twins make using some straws and marbles?

Objectives

To learn to think about what is expected to happen.

To begin to understand that '**pushes**' as **forces** can make things speed up, slow down or **change direction**.

To begin to explain how an object moves.

You will need

Straws; marbles; large sheets of paper with as rough a surface as possible or chalk to mark out track lines, on the playground.

Preparation

Show the children a marble and place it on top of a desk. Ask them how they can make it move. Talk about forces that can push the marble and ask for demonstrations. Most children will want to flick the marble with their fingers. Talk about how they can make it change direction and how they can stop it.

Discussion and research

- Talk to the children about Mike and Mary being bored and show them the straws.
- Ask them how they can make the marble move and change direction using the straw.
- Eventually someone will realise that blowing down the straw makes it possible to start the marble **rolling**, change its direction and make it stop.
- Ask them to work out how they could play 'blow football' in pairs using a desktop. They will need goals and a few simple rules.
- Ask the pair with the clearest rules and the best technique to demonstrate to the rest of the class.

Obtaining evidence

- Tell the children that Mike and Mary didn't play blow football but they made up a race game using the marbles, straws and large pieces of paper.
- *What do you think they did?* The discussion needs to focus on each person having a marble and blowing it around a track.
- Draw some tracks on the whiteboard. For example, a straight track will be far too easy and one with too many tight bends will be far too difficult.
- When they know and understand what kind of track will work, give each pair a large piece of paper (or use the playground) so they can draw their track.
- Tell them that this is the kind of game Mike and Mary made up.
- Let each pair race their marble against one another.

Drawing together

- Find someone who can really control their marble and ask them to demonstrate to the rest of the class.
- Ask them whether they think Mike and Mary enjoyed playing this kind of game.
- Remind them of what pushes the marble and how it can be made to stop and change direction.

Further ideas

Collect objects that roll and ask questions about what is the best shape for rolling along a tabletop. Ask the children how they can move a heavy book across their desktop without just lifting it up and putting it down. They will have to roll it, push it or drag it. Collect lots of different toys and ask the children how they move.

Support

Some children will find that keeping the marble on their racetrack is very difficult. They may need to line the side of the track with books so that the marble bounces off them rather than rolling off the paper. It is important to keep the tracks simple but interesting. This will need the help of as many adults in the classroom as possible.

Extension

If the paper is too **smooth** the marble will roll too quickly. Of course, if the paper is too **rough**, it will be difficult to make the marble move at all. Some children will enjoy finding the 'best' paper. The shape of the track will help make the game more enjoyable. Is there a 'best' track? Ask the children what they think. *Which one makes the game the most interesting?* Some children might think about crazy golf and want to make a miniature course to use with their marble.

Scientific language

push – to move an object away from oneself, or the source of the force.
rolling – moving by rotating over a surface, like a car wheel.
force – power exerted on an object.
smooth – uneven, with no bumps.
rough – uneven and bumpy to touch.
change direction – to start to move towards a different target.

The world's best parachute

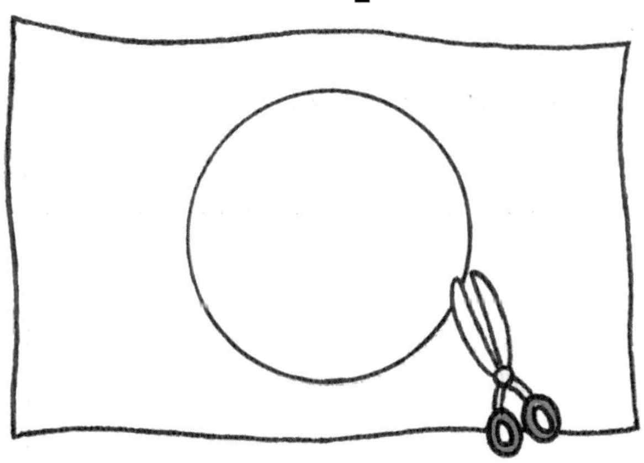

- Draw your parachute.

Can you explain why your parachute worked?

What problems did you have when you were testing it?

Whose car goes the furthest?

- Draw how you think you can help Mike and Mary's cars to travel further.

What were the results when you tested the car on the ramp?

How high is the ramp?	How far does the car go?

What will you say to Mike and Mary to stop them arguing?

The lorries and the steep hill

- Look at each of these examples of 'friction'. Draw an arrow to where you think the friction is working and say whether it is 'helpful' or 'not helpful'.

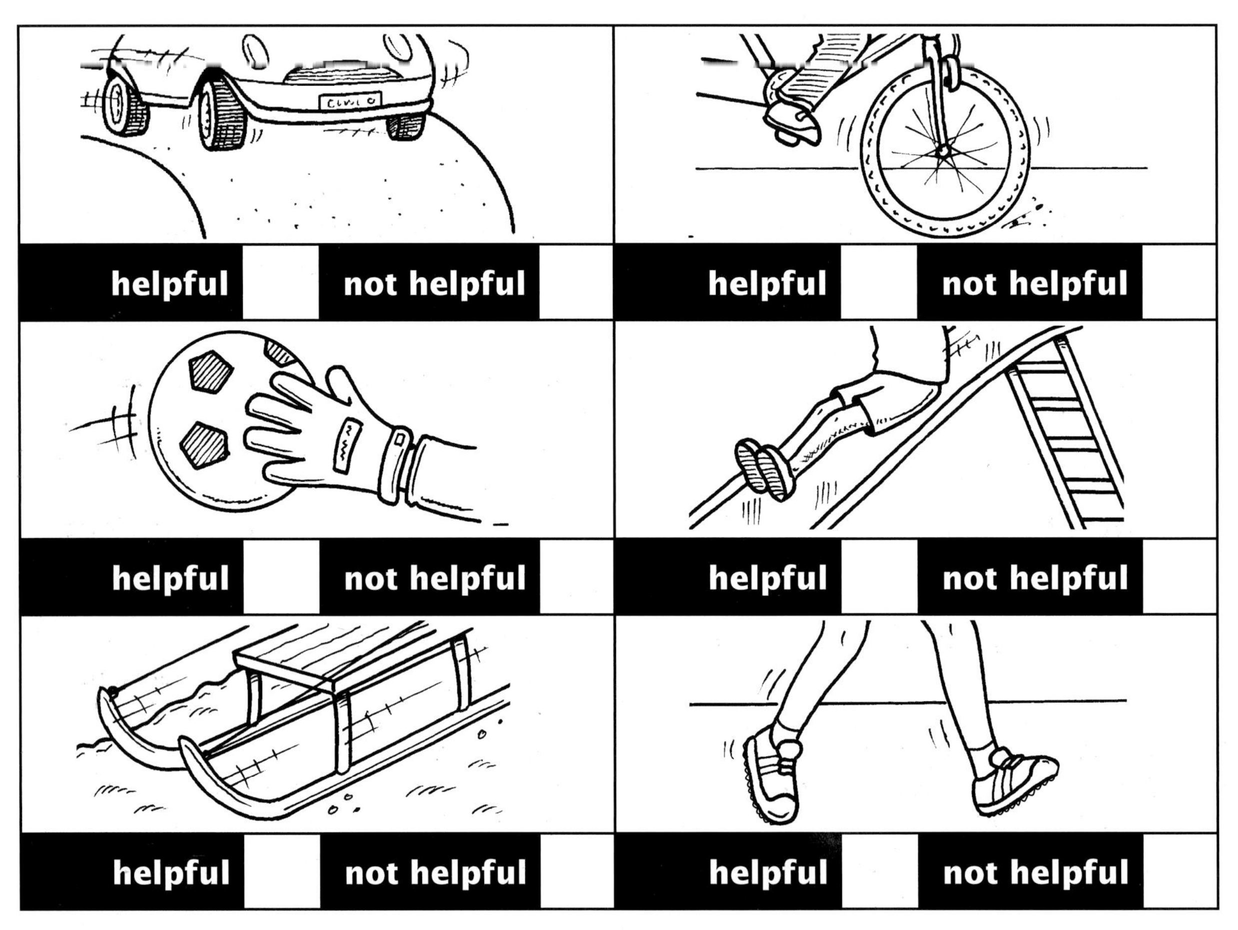

Which material do you think will be best to stop the lorry.

___

Why do you think that it will work best?

___

Were you right? What would you tell Bessie Buildit?

___

___

SCHOLASTIC
www.scholastic.co.uk

Chapter Four

Grouping and changing materials

This chapter contains seven lessons aimed at showing that different materials have different properties, and that their suitability for various jobs depends on which properties they possess.

In **The best bubbles in the world!** children carry out an experiment to create bubbles using different types of wand, bubble mixture and technique. This helps them to understand what bubbles are, and also introduces them to the idea of choosing and using appropriate materials for a task.

If they have completed Chapter Two, the children will already be familiar with soil as a source of nutrients for plant life. **What is soil?** allows a closer examination of the components of soil, in an experiment which shows how composition of soil can vary greatly from place to place.

Cleaning the king's money provides an opportunity to learn about the characteristics of four common liquids, and the concepts of acids and dissolving, with further reinforcement of the importance of fair tests.

The next four lessons all focus on choosing materials that are appropriate for various tasks. **Mopping up** requires the children to think about the different properties of a range of cloths, with an experiment to show which of the cloths is the most absorbent. **Nest building** adds to what the children have already learned about the conditions necessary to sustain life, but this time in the context of choosing appropriate materials based on the amount of insulation that they provide. **Shoelaces** requires children to assess the strength and flexibility of different materials and also introduces the idea of changing materials by twisting, bending or stretching them. **Wrapping parcels** again requires assessment of flexibility and strength, but for a very different purpose.

Seven photocopiable pages are provided for the recording of the results, in this chapter.

The best bubbles in the world!

Setting the context

Yesterday Uncle George gave Mike and Mary two huge containers of bubble mix but now they had used it all up and also lost the wands that made the bubbles. When their mum saw that they were sad she had an idea and she said, 'Cheer up! Let's see if we can make our own bubbles.'

The problem

Can we make our own bubble mixture? Does it matter how we blow into the wand? What shape of wand will make the best and the biggest bubble?

Objectives

To learn to observe, ask questions and conduct an experiment.
To know how to record findings.
To be able to explore how materials can change when **mixed** and can change shape under different processes.

You will need

A copy of photocopiable page 72 for each group; plastic containers marked in millilitres; washing-up liquid (good quality); water; glycerine; standard wands for testing the bubble mixtures; different thicknesses of wire including pipe cleaners and long art straws; painting aprons; washing-up bowls.

Preparation

You need four 500ml containers with the following combinations of washing-up liquid and water, with the same amount of glycerine (1 per cent) added to each one.

Container 1: 40 per cent washing-up liquid;
Container 2: 30 per cent washing-up liquid;
Container 3: 20 per cent washing-up liquid;
Container 4: 10 per cent washing-up liquid.

Discussion and research

- Talk about the problem that Mike and Mary have.
- Find out what the children know already about bubbles. For example, they should be able to describe how to blow them, what they have used in the past and the colour and shape of bubbles.

Obtaining evidence

- Each small group should work outside, wearing painting aprons and using the same standard wand. Everyone should have a chance to blow the bubbles and talk about what they need to record in the boxes.
- Give them photocopiable page 72 and talk about what they need to do.
- Container 4 should make the best bubbles. When all the groups have finished, ask them which is the best way to blow through the wand. Show them that it is also possible to drag the wand slowly and smoothly through the **air**.
- Ask some children to demonstrate that a slow smooth breath works best.
- Talk to them about what shape of wand might make the biggest bubble and show them the wire, pipe cleaners and straws.
- Ask each group to make three wands. Limit the diameter of the largest to

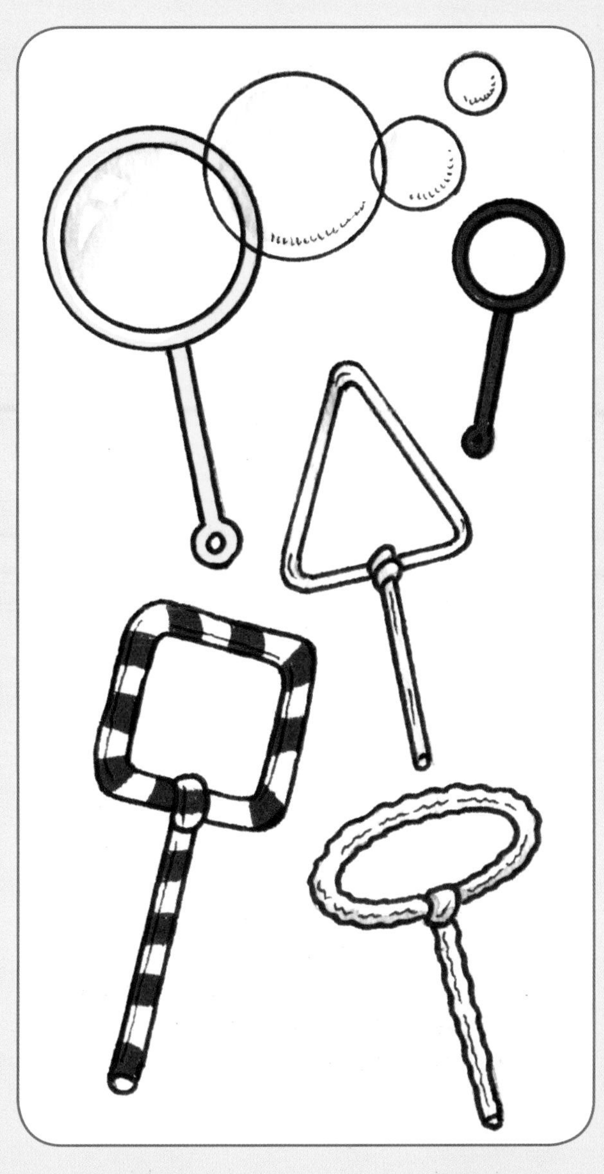

approximately 15cm. If it is **square**-shaped, each side should be no bigger than 15cm. The wands should be made out of different materials.

- Make a large quantity of bubble mixture (10 per cent washing-up liquid). Some of it will need to be in washing-up bowls for the larger wands.
- Find out which size and shape and material, e.g. thick wire, thin wire, pipe cleaner, etc. makes the biggest **floating** bubbles.

Drawing together

- Ensure that the children understand their results (that bubbles need a particular mixture and method of blowing the wand).
- Talk to the children about the shapes and sizes of the bubbles and demonstrate their best ones.
- Ask them to think carefully about the materials that made the wands and which thickness of wire worked best.
- Talk about the materials the bubbles are made from. Ask the children what they think. Each bubble consists of two thin films of soap with water in between. This is why the right mix is important.
- Ask them to look at the colours of the bubbles which will be like a **rainbow**.

Further ideas

What difference does the weather make to how bubbles float through the air? Do large bubbles float longer than smaller ones? Why do they not float forever?

Support

Some children will need help constructing the wands and blowing through them. All children will need to be calm enough to blow properly to make the bubbles as well as watch them closely.

Extension

Use prisms to make rainbows and relate these to the colours in the bubbles. Some children will be able to mix the correct colours and paint a rainbow. Use 10 per cent of extremely cheap washing-up liquid. Does it make a difference?

Scientific language

mixing – stirring different substances together.
rainbow – the colours that are made when white light is split into its spectrum colours.
square – a shape with four sides of equal length.
float – hang in the air, or water, without sinking.
air – the mixture of gases all around us.

What is soil?

Setting the context

The twins, Mike and Mary, are helping their mum plant some seeds in the garden. They are digging and raking and their mum keeps telling them that the soil must be really fine so that the seeds will grow properly. After they had been helping for quite a long time, Mike suddenly turned to his mum and said, 'What is soil? What's it made from? Is it all the same?' 'Well', said his mum, 'What do you think? Shall we try to find out?'

The problem

How can their mum show them that soil is made up of different layers and that if you collect soil from different parts of the garden, the layers could be very different?

Objectives

To know how to record observations of materials.
To begin to understand that materials are sorted in different ways.
To learn to observe, ask questions and conduct a fair test.

You will need

Dry soil from two different parts of the school grounds; magnifying glasses; containers such as one-litre plastic soft drink bottles with their tops cut off; water; something to stir the soil with (dowel, large spoon, etc.); a copy of photocopiable page 73 for each child.

Photos © Peter Rowe

Preparation

Show the children some dry soil. Let them touch it and look at its **particles** closely using their magnifying glasses. Ask what they think it is made of and record their answers on the whiteboard.

Discussion and research

- Give each small group the two different samples of dry soil and ask them to separate each sample into different parts. They should find large and small pieces of grit, pebbles, twigs, bits of vegetation and even the odd insect.
- Ask them to suggest ways of recording what they see and how they might display their experiment.
- Ask them whether they think that the soil samples are different and whether they know enough about what soil is made of to tell Mike and Mary.

Obtaining evidence

- Give each small group two plastic containers, two samples of different dry soil and something to stir the soil and water mixture with.
- Put about 4cm of each soil sample, into their containers and cover with plenty of water, ensuring the soil is submerged.
- Each sample needs to be stirred well and then again about two hours later and then again the next morning. They then need to be left, undisturbed, for at least two days.

Drawing together

- After the soil and water **mixture** has been left for two days, give each child their own copy of photocopiable page 73 and ask them to look at each of their soil samples.
- They can complete the photocopiable page but it is also important to look at the **layers** of sediment and to talk again about what they think soil is made of, because they should be able to see the grit and pebbles at the bottom and the different layers of fine sand-like material **suspended** in the water.
- Give them the opportunity to talk about the differences in their soil.
- What will they tell Mike and Mary about soil?
- Why did Mike and Mary's mum want the soil to be fine before she planted her seeds?

Further ideas

This idea can be taken further by mixing a large amount of salt with some soil. When the children mix the soil and salt mixture with water, they can filter it through filter paper and then leave the water to evaporate. It will leave salt crystals that can be looked at under the microscope. Using this idea will also demonstrate the concept of dissolving.

Support

Some children will need help with the vocabulary, especially if they are using words such as sediment, suspension, etc. They will also need help in expressing their ideas when they are describing their soil. All the children will need reminding not to touch their soil samples after they have been left in the water. They really do need two days to settle so that you can see the different layers.

Extension

If you have microscopes that are relatively easy to use, they will open up a whole new world of sand **grains** and minute insects. Drawing these will produce a brilliant display.

Scientific language

mixture – two or more substances stirred together.
particles – the tiny parts that make up a solid, liquid or gas.
layers – different parts on top of one another.
suspended – hanging.
grains – a particle of salt or sand, for example.

Cleaning the king's money

Setting the context

King Greedy is really worried. His friend, King Lotsofcash, is coming to visit and King Greedy wants to boast about how much gold he has. But he has been playing with his money so much that when he looks into his collection of purses and wallets, he finds that all his coins are dirty and dull.

The problem

He can't boast to his friend if his cash doesn't look clean and bright. What can King Greedy do to make his money shiny?

Objectives

To learn to observe, ask questions and conduct a fair test.
To be able to predict and then record what happens.
To begin to understand how one **material** (an acid) can change another.

You will need

1p and 2p coins that are dirty and stained (DO NOT use old coins that have any value because what happens to them would make them worthless); four see-through containers; vinegar, cola, lemon juice and diluted orange squash; sieves; paper towels; running water; a copy of photocopiable page 74 for each child.

Preparation

Organise the children into small groups and give each group four containers with each of the **liquids** in. You only need enough to cover the coins. The children should write labels for each container with the name of the liquid on – vinegar, cola, lemon juice and orange squash. Tell them that they are going to help the king find the best way to clean his coins.

Discussion and research

- Allow the children to taste each of the liquids and to try to describe the tastes. (To meet most school's Health and Safety risk assessments, they could, with adult supervision, dip their clean fingers into each liquid. It is important to check the school's Health and Safety policy and decide whether it is appropriate to tell parents what the experiment involves.)
- Talk about some liquids being **acids**. You should specifically name vinegar (ascetic acid) and lemon juice (citric acid).
- Ask the children what they think might happen if you put the coins in the liquids. Also ask them why.
- If possible, lead the discussion on to talking about the acids '**dissolving**' or changing the material (the dirt) on the coins.

Obtaining evidence

- Give out the coins and tell the groups to carefully put two coins into each of their containers.
- Give each child a copy of photocopiable page 74 and ask them to complete the first sentence.
- After an hour, they need to look at their containers and describe what is happening.

- Ask them to talk about and describe what they see to you and to each other before they complete the second part of photocopiable page 74.
- After 24 hours, use the sieves to carefully wash the coins and dry them on the paper towels.
- Make sure the children know what liquid the coins came from. Don't let them get the coins mixed up.

Drawing together

- Show them some coins that have not been in any liquid to remind them how dirty they were.
- Talk to the children about what they can see has happened to their coins and discuss which of the liquids has made the coins the shiniest.
- Ask the children why and remind them that the acids have changed the dirty surface and removed the dirt.
- They can complete the photocopiable page and should be able to give King Greedy some good advice about cleaning his coins.
- Ask the children if they drink cola. (It will have made the coins shiny).
- Ask the children what they think it might be doing to their teeth when they drink a lot of it.

Further ideas

Eggshells are made of a similar material to the children's teeth. Leave some in cola for a few days and see what happens. This could lead to all kinds of discussions about drinking and eating healthily.

Support

Some children might need help in writing the labels and completing the photocopiable page. If possible, let them draw what has happened rather than writing. The names of acids might be difficult but are worth using. The more teaching assistants who are available to help wash the coins the better.

Extension

Some children might find what happened to the coins so fascinating that they will want to try other 'materials' and other 'acids'. If possible, leave a space in the classroom for more experiments, or you could leave the coins in cola for longer.

Scientific language

material – something that has special qualities that help it to do its job well.
liquids – wet materials, that can flow.
acids – a liquid that can dissolve other materials.
dissolving – when a solid mixes into a liquid and cannot be seen.

Mopping up

Setting the context

Mr and Mrs Mop are brilliant cleaners. They sweep, dust, scrub and tidy. But they have a problem. They can't buy any more of their favourite cloths for wiping up water and any other liquids that have been spilled. There are some other kinds of cloths available, but they don't know which ones to buy. What are they going to do?

The problem

Mr and Mrs Mop need to find a new material to mop up water. What is the best material to do this? Can you help them choose?

Objectives

To learn to observe, ask questions and conduct a fair test.
To know how to use a range of common materials.
To be able to choose a material for a specific purpose.

You will need

Plenty of containers or cups (transparent if possible) for **measuring** water in **millilitres** and for holding water; shallow trays; a copy of photocopiable page 75 for each child; three different **materials** (for each group) such as bought cloths and kitchen towels, crêpe paper, tissue paper or art paper, etc.

Preparation

Organise the children into small groups. Each group will need a work space, labelled samples of three materials, a tray, access to water, a container that can measure in millilitres or three cups (see Support). Give each group a copy of photocopiable page 75.

Discussion and research

● Show the children the materials and make sure that they can identify them.

● Talk to them about which cloth/material they think will work best so that they can help Mr and Mrs Mop to mop up the most **liquid**. Try to mention thickness, **softness** and **absorbency**, if possible.

● If you have one or two different kitchen towels or cleaning cloths, make sure the children look carefully at any differences.

● Ask the children which ones they think will not work very well and ask them why.

● After the discussions, ask each group to write down on their photocopiable page the material that they think will be the best for Mr and Mrs Mop.

Obtaining evidence

● Talk to the children about how they might test the materials. If the children give you some good ideas that will work, use them.

● Explain that for each material they will need to carefully spill 250ml of water into a tray and then place the material on the water (each piece of material must be on the water for the same length of time). They must then squeeze the material into the measuring container so that the amount of water the material has soaked up can be measured (see support also). It is important to demonstrate how to do this because it is quite difficult.

● Talk to the class about fair tests and ask them why it is important to use the same length of time to soak each material and the same person to squeeze the material.

● Let each group do their tests and record their results through drawing and or recording millilitre measurements. Alternatively, they could use comparative language e.g. 'holds the least' 'holds the most', 'holds more than' or 'holds less than'.

Drawing together

● When they have completed all their tests, ask each group which material will be the best for Mr and Mrs Mop to use.

● If the same result is not common to all the groups, test each of the 'winning' materials again, until there is a 'best' one.

● Ask why they think it mops up the most water.

● *What about the worst material? Why does it not work?*

Further ideas

Once the best material for Mr and Mrs Mop has been chosen, why not market it so that they will buy it? Choose different materials for packaging and design a name and logo to make it look attractive.

Support

Some children will find it difficult to measure in millilitres and will need to make direct comparisions to obtain results. They could squeeze the water from each material into individually labelled transparent containers. Adults should mark the water levels on each container so comparisons can be made.

Extension

It is likely that either a cloth or a kitchen towel will work best. The children could be encouraged to further this experiment on their own and test different cloths and kitchen towels to find out the best one for Mr and Mrs Mop. They could investigate whether expensive cloths or kitchen towels are the best.

Scientific language

liquid – wet materials, that can flow.
absorb – to soak up liquid.
measure – to work out size.
millilitres – units for measuring liquids.
material – something that has special qualities that help it to do its job well.
soft – not hard, pliable.
absorbent – able to absorb liquids.

Nest building

Setting the context

Mr Hatch was going shopping so he looked outside to see what the weather was like. He saw that it had been frosty overnight. 'I'll need my warm scarf and gloves,' he thought. 'Now where did I have them last?' He remembered wearing them when he was talking to his neighbour in the garden last week, so he went outside to look. He found his scarf and one glove lying on top of the wheelbarrow where he must have put them down. One glove was missing. He looked all around but could not find the second glove. He stood and watched to see what was happening. A few minutes later a small robin flew down from the top of his hedge and picked up his second glove, disappearing into a small hole in the hedge with it. Mr Hatch crept forward to see what the robin wanted with his gloves. He saw that the robin was using them to line its nest to help keep it warm during the winter. Mr Hatch needed his gloves just as much, so he wondered if he could find something else that would keep the robin just as warm as his gloves.

The problem

How can Mr Hatch help the robin to keep its nest warm during the winter?

Objectives

To learn to collect evidence by making observations and taking measurements.
To be able to recognise when a test is fair and unfair.
To know how to follow simple instructions to control risks to themselves.

You will need

A range of suitable **materials** to **insulate** the nest; small glass jars with lids; warm water; thermometers; stopwatches or timers (optional) for more confident learners.

Preparation

Have some water ready to pour into the jars, not too hot to touch, but not too cold, so that it does not cool down too much before the test starts.

Discussion and research

- Tell the children Mr Hatch's story.
- Ask them why they think the robin chose Mr Hatch's gloves. Decide that it was to keep its nest warm, during the winter.
- Set the children the problem of finding a material for the robin to use to line the nest so that Mr Hatch can have his gloves back.
- Agree on the materials that could be used instead.

Obtaining evidence

- Organise the children into groups, according to their suggested material and ask them

jar of water to represent robin

cotton wool

to think of a way that they could test out whether their material will keep the nest the warmest.

- Agree together that they need to build a nest and that they need to keep something warm, for the longest amount of time.
- When the children have thought about how they could test out whether theirs is the best material, gather together as a whole class to think through the possibilities.
- Agree that the nests will have to be the same shape and size, and that each one will need to be made from the same amount of material, in order to make the test fair. The only thing that must be different is the type of material being used to line each of the nests.
- Agree to use small jars of warm water in order to represent the 'robin'.
- Decide how to conduct the test. The children should wrap each 'robin' in a nest and then wait for two minutes. They can compare how warm the 'robins' are by feeling the heat of the jar, and deciding if one jar is colder than another. They should then quickly return each of the jars (robins), to their nests, and wait for an additional two minutes. The children should repeat this process until they have a winner or winners.

Drawing together

- Ask the children to conclude which material made the best replacement nest for Mr Hatch's gloves. *Which material will help to keep the robin warm, during the winter? How do you know?* Disuss with the children whether their predictions were right and whether they thought their investigation was fair?
- Talk to the children about how they could improve their investigation so that they can make the nest even warmer. Collect the children's ideas so that they can be investigated another time. The children might suggest that the robin could use a different type of material or shape of nest and that the robin could build its nest in a different location next time.

Support

You will need to structure the test for some of the children, by telling them what they are going to find out and how they are going to do it. After the testing is complete, focus on the children telling you what they found out and whether their material kept the nest warm.

Extension

Ask some of the children to compare their material with Mr Hatch's gloves. Ask an adult to help them measure the temperature in each nest, at two-minute intervals, using suitable thermometers. They could then record the temperatures in a list and use these measurements to decide which nest is the best. You may also wish to introduce stopwatches or timers to measure the time intervals.

Scientific language

insulate – keep warm or cold.
material – something that has special qualities that help it to do its job well.

Shoelaces

Setting the context

Scott got up late and so he needed to get ready for work in a hurry as usual. He was fairly well organised and always had his clothes in just the right spot so that he could put them on quickly. As he was doing up his shoelaces, one of them broke. He looked in the drawer for a spare one but when he noticed there were none there, he realised that he had used up his last one a while ago and had forgotten to buy some more. What was he going to do now? He hadn't got time to go to the shop and he had no other shoes to wear.

The problem

What could Scott use instead of a shoelace to do up his shoes?

Objectives

To know how to sort **materials** according to their **properties**.

To be able to recognise and name common types of materials.

To understand that some materials are chosen for specific uses based on their properties.

To understand that some materials can be changed by twisting, bending and stretching.

You will need

Materials suitable for making laces including string, garden wire, ribbon, wool, cotton thread, elastic; shoes with lace holes; photocopiable page 76 or page 77 (for more confident learners).

Preparation

Cut the materials to a suitable length, ready for testing and threading through the lace holes.

Discussion and research

- Ask the children what Scott could use instead and why.
- Look at a shoelace and note its properties.
- Decide on the properties of shoelaces. They need to be: thin enough to fit through the holes, long enough to cover the length of the shoe and to do up securely, **flexible** enough to turn corners, and strong enough to hold the shoe in place and not snap.

Obtaining evidence

- Show the available materials and note those which the children have already suggested. Draw their attention to those materials which they have not mentioned. Ask them if they think each one will be suitable, and why or why not.
- Start to complete the chart on photocopiable page 76 together, noting each one's thickness, flexibility and strength. **Hypothesise** whether each material will make a good shoelace.
- Put the children into groups. They should test out each material by seeing if it is thin, bendy and strong enough to be used as a shoelace.
- Ask the children to give each material a mark out of ten on their individual charts and then use the information to say which material is the best.

Drawing together

- Compare each group's results and decide together which is the best substitute for Scott's shoelace. Look at the data and note together that the one that is the best has the properties needed for a good shoelace. It fits through the holes, is flexible enough to turn and twist and is strong enough to hold the shoe together without snapping.
- Ask the children to say if any materials could be made more flexible. *Could any be made stronger? How?* Use the new hypotheses to set up another investigation.

Support

Give some of the children the string, wool and plastic thread so they can conclude that the string is best because it is more bendy than the garden wire and has more strength than the wool.

Extension

When some of the children have found out which is the best material to replace the shoelace and why, ask them to test out whether they can make the wool strong enough, the garden wire more flexible or the ribbon thin enough to make an effective shoelace.

Scientific language

material – something that has special qualities that help it do its job well.
flexible – will bend without breaking.
properties – qualities that help something do a good job.
hypothesise – make a guess based on what we know.

Wrapping parcels

Setting the context

Mrs Fairlywellorganised was very pleased with herself because she had bought her friend's Christmas present in plenty of time to send it to Australia. Knowing this, she decided to wrap it on the evening before the last posting date. She went to the cupboard where she kept her wrapping paper only to find she had used it all last year. It was too late to go to the shop because it was closed and she needed to send the present first thing in the morning. She had some brown paper to make the parcel secure but really wanted to make the present look attractive as well. She hunted around the house and found a few alternatives she could use, but which one would be best?

The problem

How can we help Mrs Fairlywellorganised to choose the most suitable material to wrap her present?

Objectives

To know how to sort **materials** according to their **properties**.
To be able to recognise and name common types of materials.
To understand that some materials are chosen for specific uses based on their properties.

You will need

Sorting rings; labels for 'attractive', '**flexible**' and 'strong'; small boxes such as empty cereal packets; fabric; plastic sheeting; foil; cardboard; wood; bubble wrap; newspaper; ribbon; scissors; sticky tape; a copy of photocopiable page 78 for each pair.

Preparation

Cut the materials to the right size for the boxes being used as presents.

Discussion and research

- Talk about why we wrap presents – to make them attractive; to hide the present so

© Peter Rowe

Drawing together

- Decide as a class which is the best material to choose based on the properties considered.
- Ask the children if they can think of any other material that they could use if it were available.
- Consider whether they could make any of the materials more attractive, more flexible or stronger to make it the 'best'.

that when it is opened the recipient gets a surprise; to make the present secure.

- Identify the properties the wrapping material should have – attractive, flexible in order to turn corners, strong in order to hold the present securely inside.
- Look at the materials Mrs Fairlywellorganised found in her cupboard and name them, e.g. plastic, metal, fabric, wood and paper.
- Sort the materials into sets according to whether they are attractive, flexible and strong. Use overlapping sets when some materials can be sorted into more than one set.
- Model how to work with a partner to help each other wrap the present and draw conclusions to record on the photocopiable page.

Obtaining evidence

- Set the children off to test out their **hypotheses** by asking them to wrap their 'presents' in each of the materials. They should also complete photocopiable page 78, giving each material a tick or a cross according to how attractive, flexible and strong it is.
- Talk to each group to make sure their conclusions are based on how easy or difficult it is to wrap the boxes, whether the final present looks attractive and whether the wrapping material tears easily.

Support

You may want to organise the children into mixed-ability groups. Ask them to work with a partner to wrap and test out one material each. Every five minutes, visit each group to check that everyone is involved in the discussions and the wrapping activity.

Extension

Challenge the more confident learners to spend five minutes considering how to make foil stronger. Challenge them to use foil to make the present attractive and strong enough to withstand the postal process.

Scientific language

material – something that has special qualities that help it do its job well.
flexible – will bend without breaking.
properties – qualities that help something do a good job.
hypothesis – a guess based on what we know.

The best bubbles in the world!

- Use each of the four containers and try to blow four bubbles each time. When the bubbles work, tick a box for that container. If the bubbles don't work, put a cross.

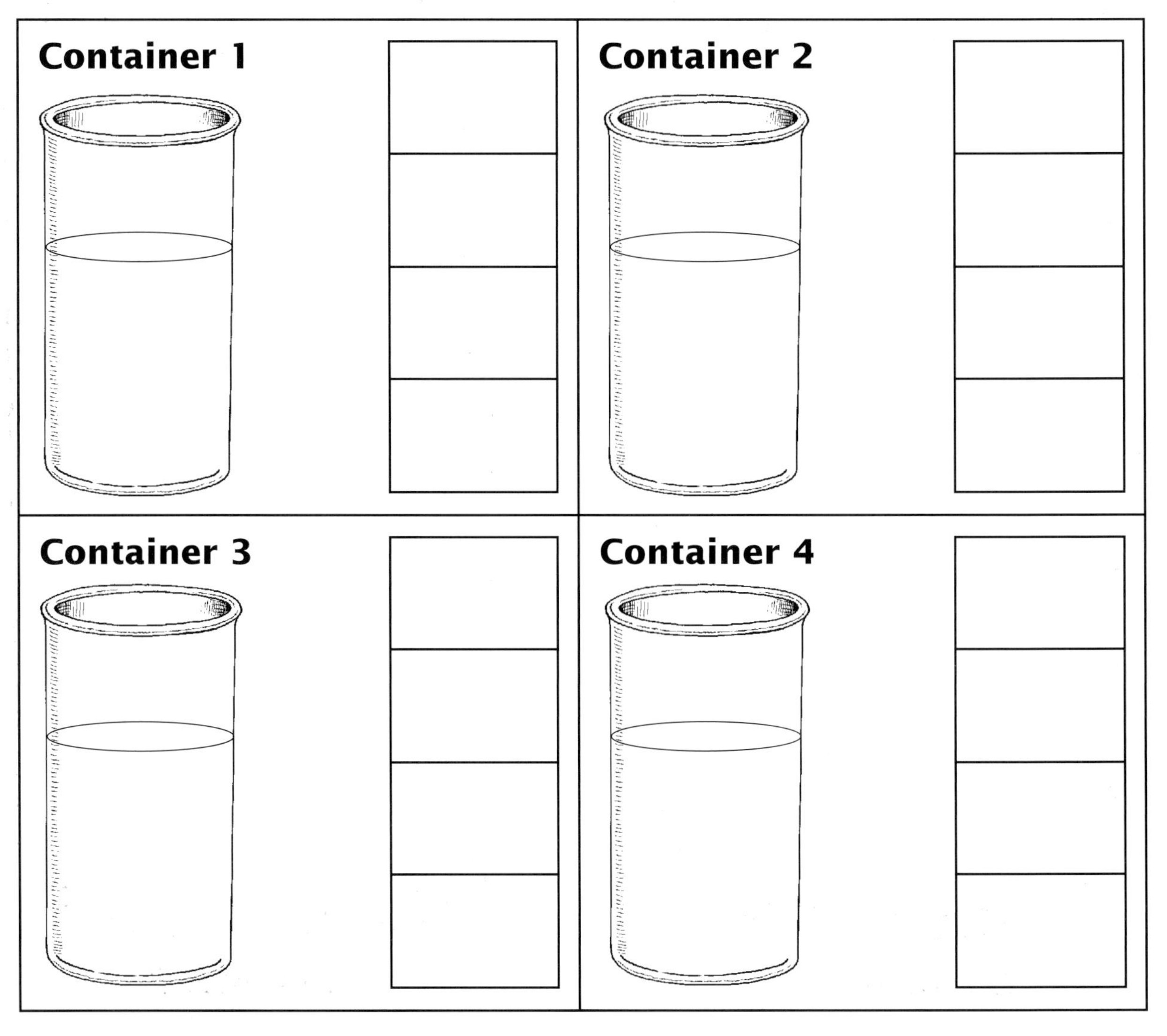

Write the missing number in this sentence:

Container ☐ makes the best bubbles.

Colour in the liquid in the container that makes the best bubbles.

SCHOLASTIC
www.scholastic.co.uk

What is soil?

- Leave the soil to settle for a few days. Describe what has happened to it.

____

- Draw what you see in each of your containers:

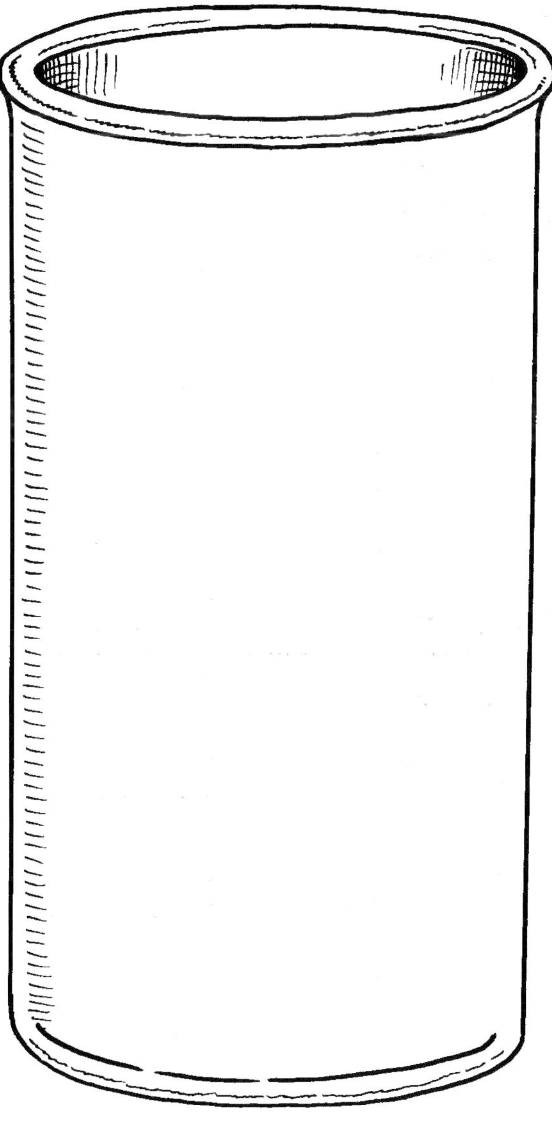

Container 1

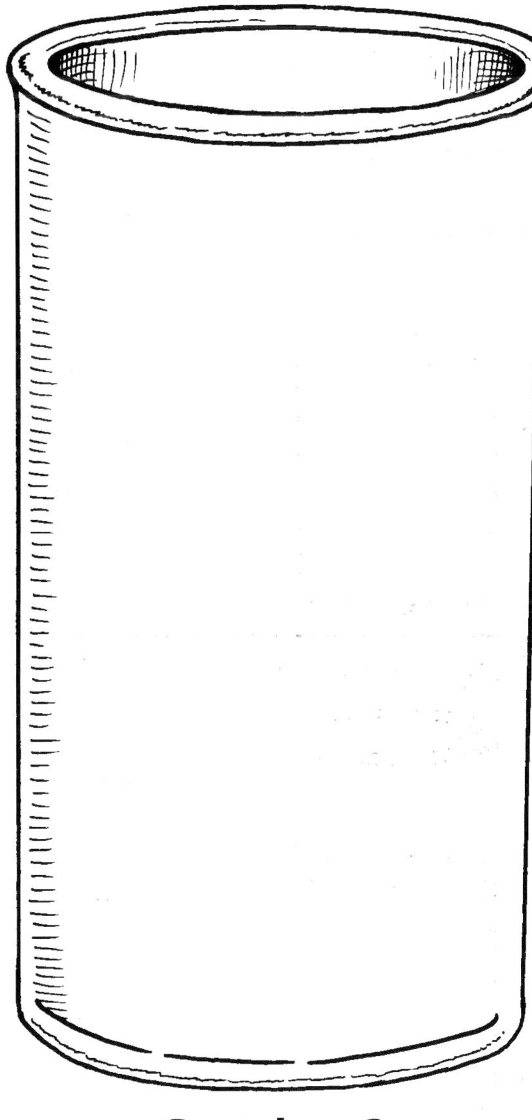

Container 2

How many layers can you see in Container 1? ____________

How many layers can you see in Container 2? ____________

Are the two soils the same? ____________

Cleaning the king's money

1. Put a ring round the liquid that will make the coins the shiniest.

Vinegar　Cola　Orange squash　Lemon juice

2. After one hour, describe what is happening to the coins in each liquid.

Vinegar	Cola	Orange squash	Lemon juice

3. After **one** day, which liquid has made the coins the shiniest? Put a ring round the correct one.

Vinegar　Cola　Orange squash　Lemon juice

4. Draw **before** and **after** pictures of the coins that are the shiniest.

Before I left the coins in	**After** I left the coins in

5. What advice would you give to King Greedy about making his coins shiny?

___

Mopping up

- Which material is the winner? Put them in order.

1st	2nd	3rd
____________ ml	____________ ml	____________ ml

____________ holds the ____________ water.

____________ holds less water than ____________ but more than ____________.

____________ holds the ____________ water.

____________ is the best material for Mr and Mrs Mop to use to mop up liquid.

Shoelaces

- Tick (✓) whether each material is thin, bendy and strong enough to make a good shoelace. Then give each one a mark out of ten.

	Thin	Bendy	Strong	Marks out of 10
Wool				
String				
Garden wire				
Elastic				
Ribbon				
Cotton thread				

Teacher's notes: For middle attainers. Remove elastic and cotton thread for less confident learners.

SCHOLASTIC
www.scholastic.co.uk

Shoelaces (extension)

- Tick (✓) whether the material is thin, flexible and strong enough to make a good shoelace and then give each one a mark out of ten.

	Thin	Flexible	Strong	Marks out of 10
Wool 1 strand				
2 strands				
String 1 strand				
2 strands				
Cotton thread 1 strand				
2 strands				

☐ strands of ________________________ will make the best shoelace because ____

Wrapping parcels

- Tick (✓) whether each material is attractive, flexible and strong enough to wrap a present. Give each one a mark out of ten.

Material	Attractive	Flexible	Strong	Marks out of 10

Chapter Five

Electricity, light and sound

This chapter consists of seven lessons, which teach children about simple electrical circuits, how sound is produced and heard, and several concepts related to light, including reflections, shadows and rainbows.

Quiz show! poses a problem which children can solve by constructing a simple electrical circuit with a bulb. The lesson involves constructing a 'quiz machine' which lights up when the right answer is provided, allowing children to become familiar with the components that are necessary to make a circuit work.

Hot weather adds to the children's knowledge about circuits, with an experiment which requires the use of a motor and a switch to make a battery-operated fan.

The next lesson, **Shake, rattle and roll!** aims to teach children about how sound is produced, how it travels and how we hear it. It includes an experiment to find out what sort of sound travels the furthest, by making and using some basic percussion instruments and taking measurements.

The construction of a kaleidoscope, in **Making the best patterns,** familiarises children with the concepts of mirrors and reflections.**Overtaking shadows** introduces the idea of light sources, how shadows are formed and how shadows can change when light sources are manipulated. A range of effects are demonstrated in this lesson by the repositioning of lamps.

Rescue us! builds on the children's previous learning about sound, but this time the focus is on comparing visual and audible distress signals at sea. **Rainbow wonders** gives the children an opportunity to look at rainbows and learn about how
they occur, as well as their particular colour composition.

Two photocopiable pages are provided for the recording of results.

Quiz show!

Setting the context

Kev Media has had a brilliant idea for a children's quiz show. He wants to impress his boss by showing him a simple question and answer machine. If he can prove that it works, he might get the job of building a huge one that will work on television – but can he do it and will it work?

The problem

How can Kev make a simple electrical circuit that lights a bulb? What will he need and will it impress his boss?

Objectives

To know how to create a **circuit** with a **battery** and **bulb** so that the bulb lights up when the circuit is complete.
To learn to observe, explore and ask questions.
To be able to explore, test and explain circuits.

You will need

A4 thin card; metal split-pins or paper clips; masking tape; short lengths (no more than 30cm) of thin plastic-coated **wire** with each end stripped by approximately 2cm; batteries; bulbs and bulb holders; copies of photocopiable page 94 for each pair.

Preparation

The children need to know or be reminded about how a circuit works and to understand what stops it working.

Discussion and research

- Give each pair a separate bulb, bulb holder, battery and two pieces of wire.
- Tell them to make quickly a circuit that works.
- Give each pair a copy of photocopiable page 94. Read the instructions and let each pair complete the page. It will only take a few minutes.
- Talk to the children about how important it is that the circuit is complete so that the **electricity** can **flow** from the battery through the bulb and back to the battery again.

Obtaining evidence

- Explain that you are their boss and that they have to impress you with their 'lighting-up quiz machine'.
- Give them the pieces of card and tell them that they have to write down eight simple questions on one side of the card and eight answers on the other side. Draw examples on the whiteboard. Make it very clear that the answers should not be opposite the question. Simple number questions, for example, 8 + 3 or 5 x 2, are probably the easiest. Use scrap paper first before you allow them to use the card.
- The next step is for the children to push split pins through the card or paper clips alongside each question and each answer and then to connect up each question and answer on the back of the card using the wire and masking tape (see diagram on page 81).
- The bulb and the battery need to be connected with the ends of the wires ready to touch the question and right answer to complete the circuit. This part of the activity will work much better if teaching assistants make sure the children are making the right **connections**. Use masking tape to connect the wires to the battery securely.

Drawing together

- Have they made a question and answer machine to impress their boss? Tell each pair that they have a few minutes to test their machine and make sure that it works.
- Go round and test each machine. You are the boss so be really impressed!
- Let them test their machines on each other.
- Ask them why they work. They should know that the right answer to the question completes a circuit and that the wrong answer means that there is a break in the circuit and the bulb won't light up.

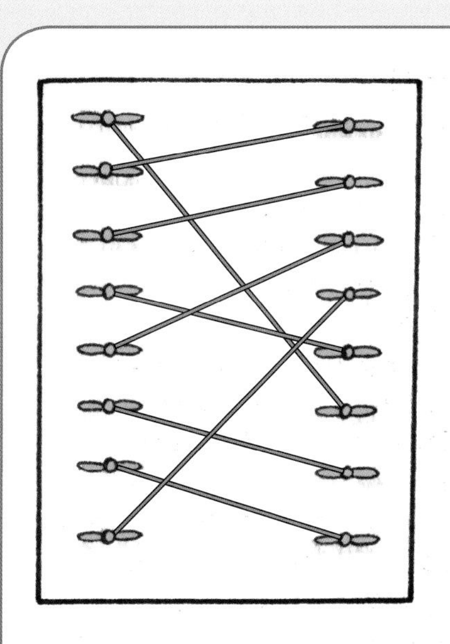

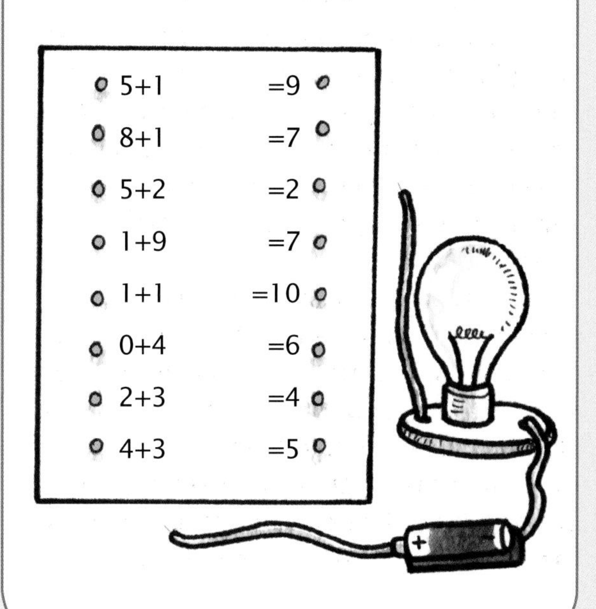

Further ideas

You could build circuits which include bells or buzzers instead of bulbs, in order to make the quiz machines even more interesting for the children to play with.

Support

This whole activity is great fun but it does needs the children to be well coordinated. The more adults there are in the classroom the better, because most children will need support with linking their connections, formulating appropriate questions and then matching these questions to the *right* answers. Some children may prefer to use paper clips instead of split pins and may find it easier to make up fewer questions for their quiz machine.

Extension

The class could make a wall-mounted 'quiz machine' which includes many more questions, on all kinds of subjects. More confident learners would also enjoy making up their own, larger machines, on their favourite topics and with longer written questions.

Scientific language

circuit – wires and a battery providing a small amount of electricity to make something, such as a bulb, work.
battery – small object that provides small amounts of electricity.
bulb – the light in a circuit.
wires – connect the different parts of a circuit, such as battery to bulb.
electricity – the energy flowing round a circuit that powers a bulb or buzzer .
flow – movement of electricity.
conduct – allow electricity to flow through.
connections – where different parts of the circuit are joined together.

Hot weather

Setting the context

It was the hottest summer on record and it was only June. How was Mary going to cope with the heat? She had no air-cooling system in her house because usually it wasn't needed. Anyway, it would be good to have something that she could carry around with her, so she could use it when she was inside or outside. What could she use to keep herself cool?

The problem

How can we help Mary make a hand-held device that would help keep her cool?

Objectives

To find out about simple **circuits** involving **batteries**, wires and motors.
To learn how a switch can be used to break a circuit.

You will need

Different kinds of hand-held, non-motorised fans; paper; stapler and staples; card; scissors; **electrical** kits to make a circuit with wire, a switch, batteries and a motor.

Preparation

Cut the paper to the right size for making hand-held, non-motorised fans. Organise the electrical equipment into sets so that each pair of children has enough to make a circuit to include a motor. Check that each set works, before the session!

Discussion and research

- Brainstorm all the different ways we can keep cool during very hot weather.
- Collect the ones that will help keep Mary cool easily when she is inside and out.
- Agree that she needs a hand-held device of some sort to keep cool.
- Give the children one minute to discuss with a partner their ideas for hand-held devices, before collecting their ideas.

Obtaining evidence

- Depending on the children's ideas, invite each child to make a fan by folding paper. Let each group look at one already made first, to work out how the design works before making one each by folding paper in a concertina style and stapling one end.
- Hold a mini-review to try out the fans. As the children fan themselves, talk about how they were made and whether they are efficient. How long do the children think they could keep this up? Either ask the children: *Can anyone come up with a better idea?* or *How can we make one of those fans that spin around* ***automatically****?* if this has already been suggested.
- Get out the equipment and let the children make a hand-held fan that works with a battery. They will need to think of a design for the fans to stick to the end of the motor.
- Ask them to put a switch into the circuit so they can turn the fan on and off.

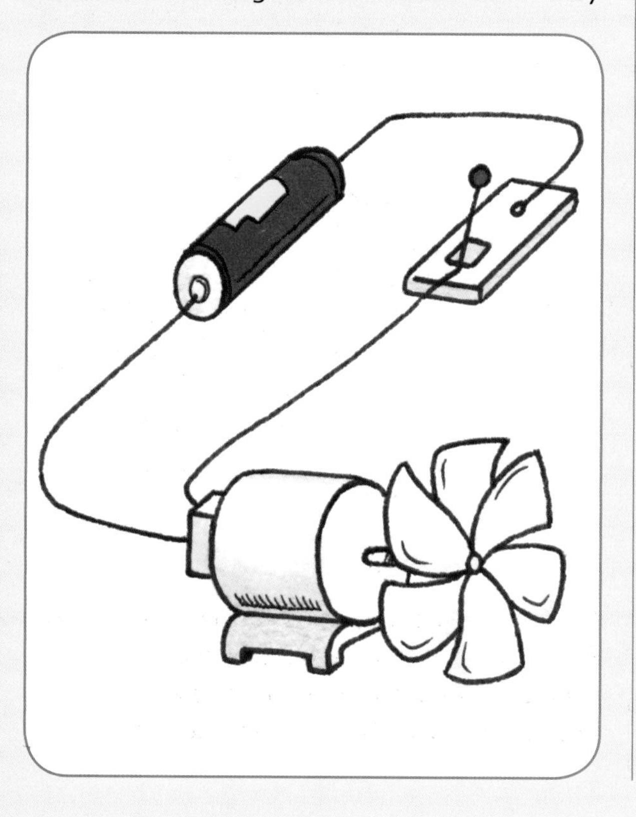

Drawing together

- Try out the battery-operated fans. Decide whether these are better.
- Look at a commercial battery-operated fan and decide what the mechanism inside will look like. *Who thinks it will be similar to the circuits you have made?*

Support

Help some of the children make their circuit so that they do not short circuit it and burn out the battery.

Extension

When the children have made their own battery-operated fans, ask the more confident learners to consider how a large, electrically-operated fan works. Give them an outline picture and ask them to draw what they think the inside looks like.

Scientific language

electrical – works by electricity.
circuit – wires and a battery providing a small amount of electricity to make something such as a bulb, buzzer or motor work.
battery – small object that provides small amounts of electricity.
automatic – works without a human action.

Shake, rattle and roll!

Setting the context

Mike and Mary's mum was fed up with them making a terrible noise. When the twins ran into the kitchen shouting and laughing, she said, 'I bet they can hear you in the next town.' The twins thought that this was quite funny but mum was serious. 'Just think how disturbing it would be if people were sitting down for dinner and all they could hear were your shouts and yells, coming all the way from here!'

Mary started thinking about this and then said to Mike and Mum, 'How far away would have to be before you stopped hearing us?' 'What?' said Mum. 'You mean how far does sound travel?'

The problem

Can you help Mike and Mary to find out? Can you make a noise using different instruments and materials and measure how far the sound travels?

Objectives

To be able to explore sounds using the sense of hearing.
To know how to make observations of sounds by listening carefully.

You will need

A selection of musical instruments, e.g. violin, clarinet, guitar, drum; cardboard tubes (similar to toilet roll tubes); a selection of dried peas, beans, lentils; masking tape; thin card; a metre measuring wheel.

Preparation

Talk to the children about what sound is and how it is made. Use the instruments to show them what **vibrates** and how you make it vibrate. Talk to them about how sound travels through the air, from the instrument to their ear. Ask them which they think will travel furthest – low sounds or high sounds and give them an example of both.

Discussion and research

- Talk to them about Mike and Mary's problem.
- Show them the tubes and the selection of dried beans and peas.
- Ask them how they could make a simple instrument that you have to shake.

- Talk to them about the different sounds lentils will make compared to dried butter beans. Demonstrate and ask them which sound they think will travel the furthest.

Obtaining evidence

- The children should work in pairs and close off one end of their tube with thin card and masking tape.

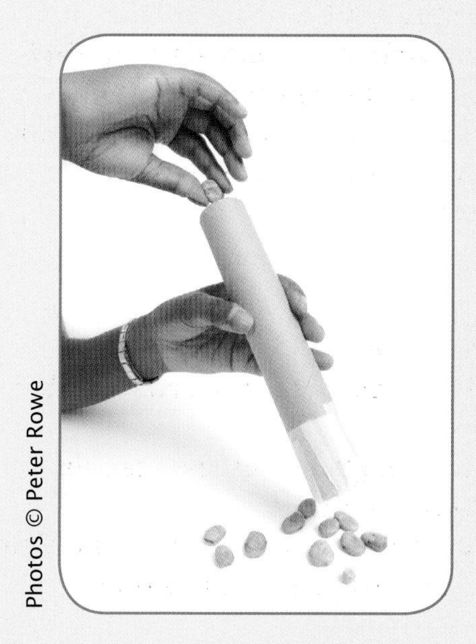

Photos © Peter Rowe

- They will then need to put an appropriate amount of their chosen peas, beans or lentils, into the tube and close off the other end.
- They can now try out their shakers.
- When they have demonstrated them to each other, ask them again which one they think will make the sound that carries the furthest.
- Ask them how they can prove this.

Drawing together

- Someone will have to listen to each instrument and gradually move further away until they can no longer hear it. The last point where they did hear the sound is the distance that has to be measured.
- To make this a fair test, the children should realise that the same person has to listen to all the instruments.
- Talk about which instrument can be heard the furthest away.
- Ask: *Why do you think this is? How would you explain the results to Mike and Mary?*

Further ideas

The ear and how it works is fascinating to children and some of them will be able to give graphic details of some of the problems they have had with their ears. Making musical instruments is also creative and enjoyable. They can be based on instruments you have to strike in some way and those with strings.

Support

Some children will need help in sealing both ends of their tubes and in selecting the right amount of dried beans, peas, etc. For example, they will need quite a lot of lentils but only a few large dried beans. The listening and measuring is quite difficult and, as usual with practical experiments, it is important to have as many adults with the children as possible.

Extension

Further experiments can be done using the instruments. For example, does a violin's high notes carry further than the low notes? Do the **sound waves** made by striking a bass drum, carry further than the sounds of a snare drum? Birdsong and the calls made by whales are also interesting to many children.

Scientific language

vibration – rapid movement from side to side.
sound waves – the way sound travels through the air.

Making the best patterns

Setting the context

The twin's uncle, Will Daubalot, the famous artist, can't seem to make colourful patterns on his latest painting. He is worried because he is supposed to have a painting ready for an exhibition in a week's time. Mike and Mary think they can help and ask their mum for some mirrors and any bright scraps from her sewing box. When they are ready, they ring their uncle and tell him to come to their house and to bring his paints, because they think they can help him. He sounds very relieved and says he is on his way.

The problem

Will the twins be able to help their uncle? Is it possible to use mirrors and bright scraps of plastic, paper and sequins to make lots of patterns and shapes? Do you think you will be able to make enough patterns to help Will Daubalot?

Objectives

To learn to think about what is expected to happen.
To learn to observe, explore and ask questions.
To be able to make observations and comparisons.

You will need

Three **mirrors** for each small group; plain paper; masking tape; sequins, beads and very small bright scraps of foil, cellophane, plastic; a copy of photocopiable page 95 for each group; digital camera (optional).

Preparation

Organise the class into small groups. Give each small group a mirror and ask them what they think it does. They should know the words 'reflect' and '**reflection**'. If they don't, tell them the words. Talk about how the 'reflection' gets into the mirror – how does it work? They should understand the science: for example, that **light** is being reflected

© Peter Rowe

from an object such as their face or their hand and that it bounces back from the mirror. Ask them if they think the mirror would work in the dark.

Discussion and research

- Give each group a large sheet of white paper to put on the table top, one mirror and some coloured sequins and scraps.
- Let them experiment with moving the scraps around and making different patterns on the white paper.
- Give each group another mirror and ask them whether they can make more complicated patterns by using the mirrors in different ways.
- Help them to stand them at right angles to each other with the sequins, etc. between the mirrors.
- Ask some of the groups to demonstrate their patterns and to explain to the class what they did.

Obtaining evidence

- Tell them about Will Daubalot's problem and ask them how they can help the twins.
- Give each group a third mirror and let them experiment. Tell them that they have to find a way to make the best and the most beautiful pattern.
- Give each group a copy of photocopiable page 95 and help them to make a kaleidoscope.
- Tell them that they have to move the sequins, etc. to make the best patterns.
- They will need the photocopiable page to draw, in colour, their two best patterns.

Drawing together

- Which pattern do they think Will Daubalot would like to use for his painting?
- Make sure that each group can share their patterns with the other children.
- If you have a digital camera, the patterns will make interesting photographs that can be changed even more using a program such as Adobe Photoshop®.

Further ideas

This kind of activity provides all kinds of cross-curricular links. The kaleidoscope patterns can be used for all kinds of artwork, from paintings to collages. Building bigger, better and more original kaleidoscopes could be an interesting design and technology problem.

Support

Some of the scientific concepts relating to reflection are quite difficult and may need to be simplified and repeated. Also, some children will need help in making their kaleidoscope and using it. If there are too many sequins and small shapes, the pattern will be too complicated. Once again, it will be useful to have as many adults in the classroom as possible.

Extension

Many children will be fascinated by reflection and all the patterns that can be made. If you use prisms, these create even more fascinating patterns. It is possible to use white light and a prism to create a rainbow.

Scientific language

light – brightness that can be seen.
mirror – reflects images.
reflection – bouncing an image (light) back.

Overtaking shadows

Setting the context
As he was walking home one night, Mr Smith noticed that one minute his shadow was behind him, then by his side and then in front of him. Was someone following him? The path was well lit and when he looked around he saw that he was the only person about that night. Could he have more than one shadow? Did his shadow keep moving position?

The problem
How can we help Mr Smith decide whether he has more than one shadow? Does his shadow keep moving about and why?

Objectives
To be able to identify different **light** sources, including the sun.
To learn that darkness or a **shadow** is created by the absence of light.
To find out how to make simple comparisons, identify simple patterns and link cause and effect.

You will need
A strong light which can be moved to change the direction of light (an OHP will do for the 'discussion and research' introduction, and table lamps for the group investigation); a white screen positioned in front of the light; small lamps which do not get hot when touched, cast a strong light and are flexible so that the position of the light can be changed; a toy vehicle which can be pulled along and which casts a distinctive shadow; a space to move about.

Preparation
Make sure the light is strong enough to cast a shadow of a person walking in front of it. Try out the vehicle to see if it casts a strong enough shadow to change its position and shape when it is pulled in front of a light.

Carry out a risk assessment to make sure none of the lamps overheat when touched. Make 'Children do not touch' notices to put in front of the lamps.

Discussion and research
- Tell the children the story and pose the first question. *Can we have more than one shadow? What needs to be there for a shadow to be made?*
- Invite them to contribute their ideas to the whole class to begin with, and note these down. Identify with the children that there needs to be a strong light source and solid object to make a shadow. Collect all the light sources that could be used.
- Demonstrate that a shadow is formed in this way by asking a person to stand in front of the light to cast a shadow onto your white screen.
- Ask the children to look all around to see if there is one or more shadows. Talk about how the shadow is made. Explain it is because the body, which is solid, is blocking or stopping the light from reaching the screen.
- Ask the children if they can think of a way to make more shadows. *Can we do this by*

having more solid objects or more lights?

- Test this out by asking more than one person to stand in front of the light and by adding an extra light in a different position, with one person standing in between the two lights.
- Agree that it is possible to have more than one shadow when there is more than one light.

Obtaining evidence

- Give each group of five children a lamp and a toy vehicle. Explain the 'Do not touch' rule.
- Turn on each lamp and invite the children to put the toy vehicle on the table in the centre of the light cast by the lamp.
- Where is the shadow?
- Ask them to explore where the shadow is when the toy vehicle is put to one side and then the other side of the light cast. *Does the shadow change shape, size and position?*
- Ask them to explore what happens to the shadow when the toy vehicle is pulled across through the light cast. *Does the shadow change shape, size and position?*
- Draw pictures of what the children have found out. Ask one child in each group to draw a picture of what happens when the toy vehicle is in the centre of the light, another two to draw where the shadow is when the vehicle is on each side of the lamp and the other two to draw what happens to the shadow when the toy vehicle is pulled across through the light.

Drawing together

- Put the first three pictures together to show the different positions of the shadows according to where the toy vehicle was standing. Now compare the sequence of pictures of what happens to the shadow as the toy vehicle is moved across the table. *Are the shadows in the same position?*
- Invite one child to walk across in front of the light. Point out what is happening to their shadow. *What is happening to the shadow? Is it changing position as well?*
- Ask the children to try to explain what is happening to the shadow as the person or solid object moves across in front of the light. *What is the person's body doing to the light?* Explain this by asking the person to walk across again but to stop walking at different points.
- *What would happen if the person stood still and the light moved?*
- Ask the more able group to explain what they found out.

Support

Work with the children to point out the position of the shadows and ensure that they draw these accurately.

Extension

Ask an additional adult to work with some of the children and to act as the 'lamp mover' so that this group can investigate what happens to the shadow's shape, size and position when the light source is moved.

Scientific language

light – brightness that can be seen.
shadow – area of darkness caused by someone or something blocking the light.

Rescue us!

Setting the context

When the Wright family decided to go out for the day on their boat, they didn't even consider that things might not go as well as they expected. They left Port Harbour early in the morning and went to their favourite island where they enjoyed a day on the beach, playing games, having a picnic and barbecue and reading favourite books. When it was time to go home, everything was packed back onto the boat. Alas, all was not well. The battery was flat and there was no way to start the engine. The radio wouldn't work either, so there was no way to raise the alarm. How on earth were they to be rescued? Bill remembered that very soon, larger boats would be leaving Port Harbour to travel across the Channel with goods and passengers. Could they make some sort of distress signal to alert the boats that they needed to be rescued?

The problem

How can we help the Wright family make an alarm that will help them to be rescued?

Objectives

To learn that there are many kinds of sound and sources of sound.
To find out that sounds travel away from sources, getting fainter as they do so.
To understand that sounds are heard when they enter the ear.

You will need

Objects that make a range of low to high sounds; coloured paints and materials to make a banner; various light sources.

Preparation

Collect the resources you are likely to need and test some of these out to make sure some cannot be heard or seen from the distance you have available.

Discussion and research

- Set the scene. Ask the children what the Wright family could use to attract attention. Talk about distress signals used by ships, such as foghorns, lights and coloured materials.
- Ask the children to hypothesise which would be best to use. Ask the children whether they want to investigate movement, light or sound to decide which makes the most effective distress signal.
- Spend a couple of minutes talking through how to make a test fair before letting the children go off in their chosen groups to plan their investigation.

Obtaining evidence

- Let the children work in three groups to plan a test to find out how effective their chosen method of attracting attention is.
- Carry out the test. You could make a large colourful banner to be waved about, various torches with different strengths of light beams and a range of musical instruments.
- Record the outcomes. This is likely to be whether the signal can be seen or heard from a distance and a record of which one can be seen or heard the most clearly from the greatest distance available to you. Decide together to conduct the test outdoors as the family were outdoors.

Drawing together

- Talk about which is the most effective signal by identifying which one can be seen or heard from the greatest distance. Give each one marks out of ten. You will probably find that they are all pretty good so you will need to refine your test by adding an additional variable.

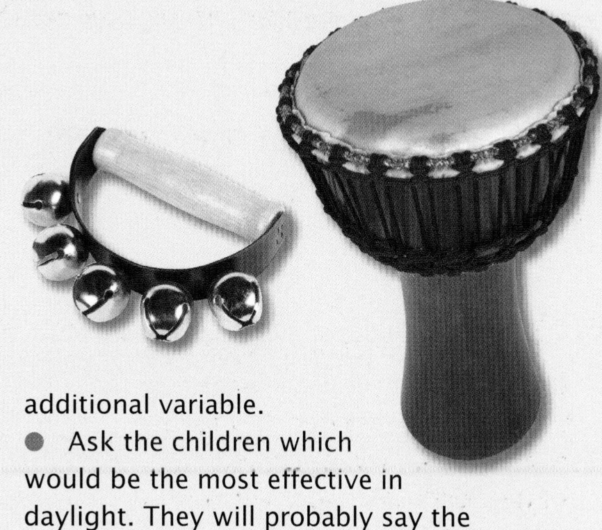

- Ask the children which would be the most effective in daylight. They will probably say the movement and the sound, because the light will not show up so much.
- Now ask them which is the most effective at night. They should say the light or sound.
- Ask them to deduce therefore which is the most effective overall. They should come up with sound.
- Ask the more able group to join you and to feed back their findings at this point.

Support

Organise some of the children into mixed-ability groups and circulate among them to make sure that all children are involved in planning and carrying out the test. Question individuals to make sure they all know what they are doing and why, and that they understand when a test is not fair.

Extension

Ask more confident groups of learners to plan and carry out a test to find out whether high or low sounds make the best distress signal. Talk about their findings and link them to how foghorns and low sounding horns are used by ships rather than high whistles.

Scientific language

sound – something that can be heard when vibrating air enters the ear.
light – brightness that can be seen.

Rainbow wonders

Setting the context

Jenna was walking home after a rainstorm one summer's afternoon. She looked into the sky and saw a rainbow. She knew why there was a rainbow but as she looked, she saw that red was at the top and violet at the bottom. Luckily for her she had her mobile phone with her and so she quickly took a photograph. When she got home, she thought, she must remember to check with other pictures of rainbows whether the red colour was always at the top or whether she should look out for different types of rainbows next time she had the opportunity.

The problem

How can we help Jenna check whether red is always at the top of a rainbow and so save her time looking for different combinations?

Objectives

To learn to decide how to find answers to a question.
To be able to talk about what happened and whether what happened was what they thought would happen.
To know how to make simple comparisons.
To be able to make decisions based on evidence.

You will need

Water; hosepipe; a sunny day; objects that refract light such as CDs, prisms, clear plastic drink's twizzlers and silver hologram paper; sticky notes; red, yellow and blue paint or ink put out into large coffee jar lids or similar so that if the colours get muddled you can easily replace them; white paper; large (2-inch) brushes; pictures of **rainbows.**

Preparation

Some time before you do the activity, try out the hosepipe to make sure you have enough space to make an arc of water and leave room for the children to stand and watch from the best vantage point to stay dry and see the rainbow as it appears. Stand with the sun to your right or your left so that the children can stand with their backs to the sun. Choose the first sunny day to do this activity. Organise the groups so that all of the children get the opportunity to do all the activities. Depending on the number of children in the class, you may need two groups of five for each one.

Discussion and research

- Ask the children when they last saw a rainbow. Talk about when this was and what was happening to make the rainbow appear.
- Agree that there has to be rain and sun to make the rainbow appear. Tell them that the rain breaks up the sunlight into its colours. Explain that the colours are always there but that we need rain to help us see them clearly.
- Go outside and use the hosepipe to make an arc of water.
- Note the colours that the eye can pick up. Note the colour that is at the top and the colour that is at the bottom of the arc.

- On return to the classroom, write down the colours of the rainbow that the children could see. Ask them which colour was at the top, which colour came next, and next and so on until you get to violet. The children may think this colour is pink because it is very close to this.

Obtaining evidence

- Organise the children into three groups to explore the colours of the rainbow. Ask one group to look in books and on the internet to see if the colours are in the same order as the ones they saw in the rainbow outside.
- Ask another group to look in the objects either by standing next to a window or going outside so that the sun can be refracted, or using a bright white light such as a powerful torch or projector.
- Ask a third group to make rainbows using just three colours. They can do this by making an arc of red, then yellow and then blue before using a paler red at the end. They will need to overlap the colours. Let them explore this for themselves to see who can work it out without mixing up all the colours. You may need to have some spare colours ready for this and the other groups so they can explore freely.

Drawing together

- Ask the children to explain to you how to make a rainbow using just the three colours. Do this as they watch. Talk about the colours and whether red is at the top. Ask them to say from their research whether they found that rainbows always have red at the top. What else can they do to check if their conclusions are right?

Support

Work with some of the children as they look at the pictures of the rainbow and label the colours using sticky notes. Help them to make rainbows of their own and talk about the colours as they mix the three colours.

Extension

Work with more confident learners on mixing coloured **light** instead of paints. *What happens when you mix red and green light?* Look at the rainbow and notice that yellow comes between red and green. Talk about the primary colours of light being red, green and blue and how the colours can still be made if these three colours are mixed. Ask them to describe their rainbow using scientific language.

Scientific language

rainbow – the colours that are made when white light is split into its spectrum colours.
light – brightness that can be seen.

Quiz show!

- Look at each of the drawings. What do you think will happen?
- Make the circuits shown in the drawings. For each one, tick (✓) the correct box to show whether the bulb lights up or does not.

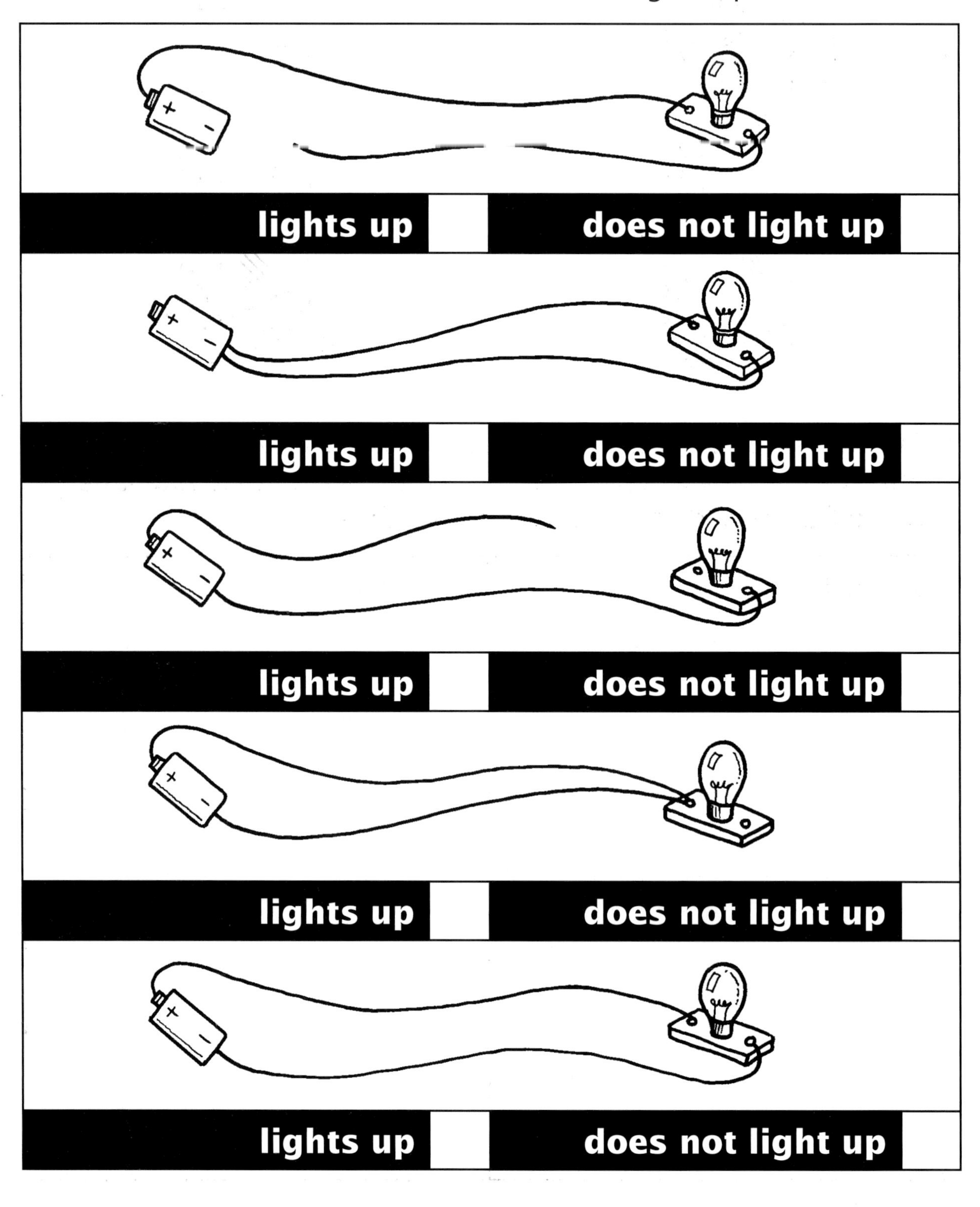

Making the best patterns

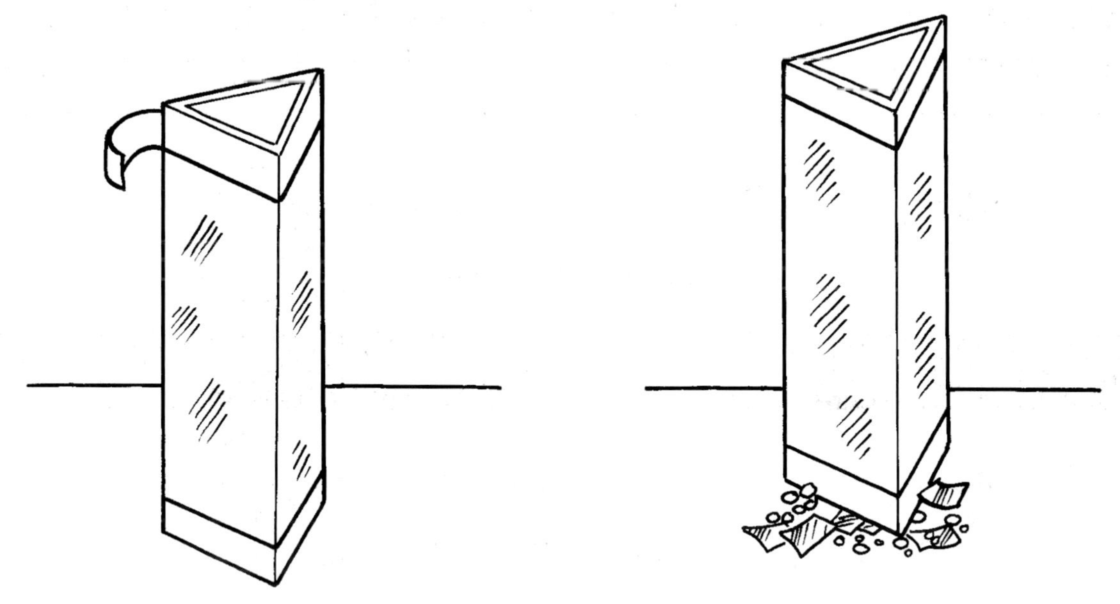

- Arrange some of your scraps on some white paper and try to draw and colour what you see. Do this twice so that you have two different patterns to show Will Daubalot.

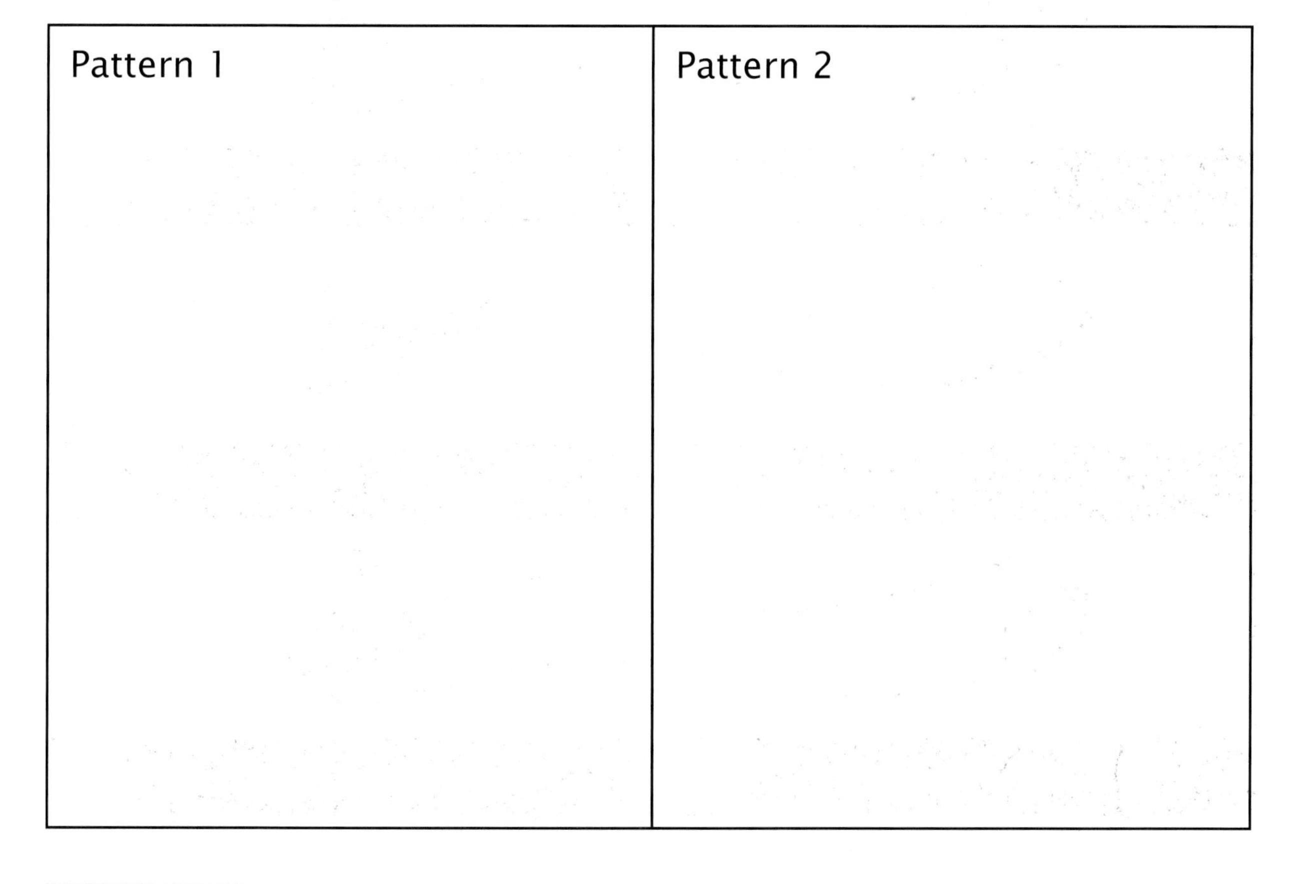

SCHOLASTIC

In this series:

ISBN 978-0439-94500-4

ISBN 978-0439-94501-1

Also available:

ISBN 978-0439-97111-9

ISBN 978-0439-97112-6

ISBN 978-0439-97113-3

ISBN 978-0439-96526-2

ISBN 978-0439-96525-5

ISBN 978-0439-96524-8

ISBN 978-0439-96556-9

ISBN 978-0439-96570-5

To find out more, call: 0845 603 9091
or visit our website www.scholastic.co.uk